HEAT

& the alchemy of food

First published in 2023

by Brolly Publishing, an imprint of Borghesi & Adam Publishers Pty Ltd

Suite 330, 45 Glenferrie Road, Malvern Vic. 3144, Australia

www.brollybooks.com | emma@brollybooks.com

This work is a collaboration between Simon Borghesi and Luisa Adam.

Recipes by Simon Borghesi, © S. Borghesi, 2023

Accompanying descriptive text by Simon Borghesi and Luisa Adam,

© S. Borghesi & L. Adam, 2023

Preface, Preliminary notes and Introduction by Luisa Adam, © L. Adam, 2023

All photographs except as otherwise noted by Simon Borghesi and Sophie Purser,

© S. Borghesi & S. Purser, 2023

Image processing by Brolly Publishing

Cover, text design, and typesetting by Emma Borghesi,

© Brolly Publishing, 2023

Additional photographs:

on pages 26-27, Photo 139887491 ©JoeGough | iStock.com

on pages 72-73, Photo 865442690 ©Kevin Lebre | iStock.com

on pages 100—01, Photo 1282375579 ©zetter | iStock.com

on pages 105, 108, 109 © Andrew Adam

on pages 146-147, Photo 510462107 ©Totajla | iStock.com

on pages 172-73, Photo 6031227 ©Phillip Minnis | Dreamstime.com

The Authors, Designer, Photographers and Publisher have
asserted their Moral Rights in this work.

All rights reserved. Printed in China.

ISBN 9781922418951

All care has been taken in the preparation of this book and to correctly attribute all contributors but neither the Authors nor the Publisher accept any responsibility for any unwitting error or oversights whatsoever. In the event any inadvertent error has occurred, please contact the Publisher to enable correction on reprint.

A catalogue record for this book is available from the National Library of Australia

HEAT

& the alchemy of food

SIMON BORGHESI

with Luisa Adam

BROLLY PUBLISHING

Melbourne

above: *vegetable plot, firepit and wood pile, backyard, Taralga*

PREFACE

THE ALCHEMY OF FOOD can mean different things, but here it refers to transformations that take place and are experienced by the senses: to the flavours, aromas, textures, sights and even sounds of food. It is about the 'magic' rather than the chemical reactions that cause them at the molecular level.

Many of the recipes within make use of age-old techniques that bring the alchemy into effect. The spell is cast during the preparation, after which the food is left on its own to, in Simon's words, 'do its thing'. And so the steak on the grill plate forms its crust, the pork in the brine softens and sweetens, the dough by the window rises, and the pickles in the jar happily ferment in the dark corners of the pantry. In much cooking practice today, there is a focus on methods and techniques, less so on the spaces in between; after all, 'watching grass grow' does not work as well on TV — but that is where the magic lies. The chef is the alchemist.

This is a timely book, woven through with themes of tradition, sustainability, simplicity, and community.

— Brolly Publishing

above: *fresh produce browse*

CONTENTS

11 Introduction
15 A Few Notes

    17 Weights, measures & temperatures
    17 Ovens
    18 Mise en place . . . or not
    18 Serving sizes
    18 Recipes
    19 Ingredients
    19 Storing foods
    21 Outdoor cooking
    24 Cooking temperatures

Vegetables | Salads

28 Pear, Walnut & Blue Cheese Salad
30 Heirloom Tomato Salad
32 Baked Asparagus with Sous Vide Egg
35 Bart's Peppers
39 Coal-Roasted Onions
42 Confit Garlic
45 Beetroot Rescoldo
47 Crushed Potatoes
51 Eggplant Escabeche
53 Gochujang Eggplant
56 Orange, Fennel & Radicchio Salad
58 Shakshuka
62 Zucchini Fritters with Smoked Salmon & Mary Rose
64 Sauerkraut

68   Pickled Fennel
69   Babaganoush

Chicken | Seafood | Duck | Trout

74   Lemon Miso Chicken with Kimchi
78   Chicken Shawarma
82   Juicy Fried Chicken
85   Chicken & Pumpkin Risotto
89   Tathra Duck
91   River Trout with Baked Potatoes & Romesco Sauce
96   Flametail Snapper with Cherry Tomatoes & Jerusalem Artichokes
99   Miso Salmon

Beef | Pork | Lamb

102   Steak Tartare
105   Ragù alla Bolognese
111   Beef Tenderloin in Miso Marinade
114   Firepit Steak with Criolla
118   Scotch Fillet with Pepper & Mushroom Sauce
121   Pulled Pork
123   Pork with Duck Rillettes
127   Smoked Pork Belly
130   Pork Roast with Crispy Potatoes, Balsamic Red Onion & Crackling

137   Lamb Loin with Salsa Verde & Potatoes
143   Rack of Lamb with Honey Glaze, Dutch Carrots
      & Beetroot Purée

Pasta | Pizza | Polenta

149   Pizza Dough
154   Pizzas
161   Focaccia
167   Carbonara Mafaldine
170   Polenta

Condiments | Sauces | Something Sweet

174   Onion Jam
176   Bronwyn's Pesto
178   Chimmichurri
181   San Marzano Sauce
183   Aioli
185   Harissa
187   Romesco Sauce
188   Basque Cheesecake
191   Chocolate Mousse

192   Acknowledgements
192   About the Authors

INTRODUCTION

BORN WITH A PASSION FOR COOKING, Simon grew up influenced on both his mother and father's side by their respect for fresh produce and their culinary skills.

His father is of Italian and Anglo-Celtic heritage, and his great-grandfather, Nello Borghesi, is credited for introducing pasta to the palates of Melbourne in the 1930s. His grandfather Bart loved to camp and cook outdoors on a campfire, always with a billy can for tea not too far away, and when in the suburbs of Melbourne to barbecue over a wood fire rather than cook indoors. Bart also surf-fished (mainly at Lorne) and trout-fished in the Tambo, Howqua, and Lachlan rivers. He occasionally hunted rabbits in the Victorian highlands, and even wild boar on the Hay Plain, near Booligal in New South Wales.

Simon's paternal grandmother was from the Considine family, wholesale butchers and meat exporters who based their business at the Newmarket Saleyards and City Abattoirs in Melbourne (operational 1897–1997).

His maternal great-grandfather Frederick Haase pioneered the snap freezing of foods in Australia. 'Seafresh Seafoods' came about in 1932 after Fred Haase and a partner experimented with freezing fish in each other's garages. Later, Fred travelled abroad and brought back with him ideas for using machinery to process fish: scaling, filleting and freezing. He then had precisely engineered equipment for this purpose manufactured in Melbourne. After building up a successful business, the Haase family sold and moved back to farming in the Gippsland region of Victoria.

As a child, Simon travelled the globe as his father was sent to different postings for his work. Although born in Australia, he moved to Texas at a very young age, where he had his first exposure to the flavours of Mexican, Central, and Southern American cuisine. Later, the family moved to the Middle East, where more culinary influences came into play, and then on to London. Simon eventually returned to Melbourne in his late teens and began studying Science at university.

Simon credits his science background for giving him a deeper understanding of the alchemy of food, which is so valuable to his cooking knowledge. He would move away from academia however, and instead take up an apprenticeship with revered chef

Jacques Reymond, and so in this way the methods and techniques of French cuisine were introduced to his already considerable repertoire.

Later, he realised a long-held dream to work under the guidance of the legendary fire chef Francis Mallmann. Travelling to South America on the wings of a whim and a hope, he by chance met Mallmann through people with whom he was staying. Mallmann offered him a job at his new restaurant in Chile, Fuegos de Apalta, where he learnt to cook over open fires, in wood ovens and on 'parillas' and 'planchas' the Mallmann way — mainly fish, lamb, vegetables, and potatoes: lots and lots of potatoes. Mallmann's fondness for this humble tuber is well known. He was also taught how to hang and smoke meats and vegetables.

A little while later, he was invited to run the kitchen at Errante Ecolodge, an exclusive ecological refuge, located in Puerto Williams, Cabo de Hornos. This is at the southern-most part of the Chilean territory, not far from the Antarctic, a remote place where Simon would serve his fare to adventurers, politicians, and well-heeled tourists alike. It was a unique experience but after some 12 months he decided it was time to resume a less isolated existence.

Returning to Melbourne, he worked at various restaurants, including Scott Pickett's Matilda and Jacques Reymond's Frederic. When Covid struck, he relocated to New South Wales and became Chef at Hugh Wennerbom's The Argyle Inn.

During this time, he built a wood-fired oven in his own backyard at Taralga and started his first solo project, Sonnie's Tuckerbox, a wood-fired pizza business like no other that he runs on weekends. It is a simple operation but the reputation for his extraordinarily delicious pizzas spreads like an excited whisper around the Central New South Wales tablelands: each is made from home-made dough, home-grown vegetables and other local produce then fired in the backyard oven.

Simon has recently taken up the role of Head Chef at Matt Moran's The Rockley Pub, some three hours west of Sydney, where he works several days and nights of the week. He then returns to Taralga, typically on a Sunday, where he lives with his partner Sophie Purser, a practising horticulturist who enjoys growing vegetables in the home garden for Simon to cook. Then he fires up the wood oven and serves fresh, hot, wood-fired pizzas to the local community.

facing page: *preparations for cooking over a firepit in Patagonia*

above: *Domino Potato, a classic Francis Mallmann dish*

'I was making this every day for about a year at Fuegos de Apalta,' recalls Simon. 'I would slice perfect rectangles and use one as a guide to cut the rest, then shave them on a mandolin and bake them in a wood oven with clarified butter, salt and thyme.'

The oven should be at about 180–200°C / 350–390°F, so it's a good one to make before the oven gets really hot for baking other dishes. Place the potatoes in a tray in the oven with some dobs of clarified butter and cover with foil. Leave them to steam up for 30 minutes, then uncover and leave them to crisp up for another 5–10 minutes. Baste regularly with clarified butter (it won't burn and will help the potatoes become crispy), and add lots of coarse salt.

A FEW NOTES

'ALCHEMY' in this book refers to the changes that occur in food after certain techniques and methods are applied: the magic of cooking. It is about those actions taken by the chef or cook that initiate a reaction which brings about a pleasing culinary result.

There are other books that cover those details far more comprehensively than is possible here, and which also explain the chemical reactions behind them in detail, but a few of the alchemical processes that pop up frequently are described below. They are all 'actions' that initiate certain results. When cooking, it is always worth keeping in mind what will happen after a certain thing is done, not putting all focus on the present.

brining, wet or dry: Although often thought of as a preservation method, the main purposes of the brines used in this book are to add moisture, tenderize, and enhance the flavour of various meats.

drying the surface: Ensuring the duck or fish skin is dry before frying, the boiled potatoes air-dried before roasting, and the steak blotted of excess moisture before grilling will result in, where meats are concerned, a nicer crust, and for vegetables such as potatoes a better crunch. A simple way to dry many foods is to leave them uncovered in the fridge.

caramelizing: By applying heat, this causes the sugars in carbohydrates to breakdown and form other compounds. The caramelization process is responsible for the crisp crunch on roast potatoes and the sweet stickiness of caramelized onions.

combinations: Mixing foods with certain other foods causes new compounds, and therefore foods, to form, with new textures and flavour, such as when oil and vinegar or butter and egg are emulsified to form a dressing or sauce.

cooling and refrigerating: This will alter the structure of food and therefore its texture: it can be as simple as 'setting' the food. On the other hand, more complex changes also take place, such as when resistant starch (a type of dietary fibre) is formed when carbohydrates including rice and potatoes are allowed to fully cool.

cooking: Boiling, baking, grilling, roasting and frying all impact on food by changing its structure through the use of heat, causing new flavours and textures and therefore foods to form.

double-cooking: This is a way to control cooking where parts of one ingredient require different amounts, such as when a potato is first boiled to cook and soften the inside, and then fried quickly at high temperature to crisp up the outsides.

fermenting: Introducing ingredients such as food acids (vinegar, lemon juice), sugars, salt, and beneficial bacteria also alters the flavours and textures of foods while providing a hostile environment to harmful bacteria, and therefore enables food to be preserved for longer periods.

hydrating: Adding moisture softens foods but can also deplete flavour.

kneading: Kneading dough forms gluten which gives bread and other dough-based foods a structure, while also providing pockets to hold air. The amount of kneading varies, depending on the desired results.

Maillard Reaction, instigating: This reaction has some similarities to caramelization processes, although more complex, and takes place when heat causes an interaction between protein (amino acids) as well as sugars. It is responsible for the crust on steak, for example.

marinating: Similar to wet-brining but with a focus on adding flavour; marinades don't usually carry the same high salt level of brines so are not as effective in tenderizing the meat, but nor are they rinsed off before cooking. While brines will typically include various aromatics, marinades will often include other ingredients such as fruit pulp.

moisture, reducing: Reducing moisture through heat and evaporation intensifies flavour and thickens texture.

resting: Resting certain foods after cooking allows them to continue to increase in temperature, so they continue to cook, but not over-cook. During resting, some foods also re-structure and become firmer as they cool down. Where meats are concerned, it also helps the juices to settle.

rubs, using: Rubs are similar to dry brines but have a greater emphasis on flavour, yet they will also season the meat and add some moisture, while helping to tenderize it.

salting: Salting food causes many changes, depending on at what stage in a recipe it is introduced. On one level, it can be used simply to enhance flavour; on other levels, it is used to draw out moisture and also to preserve foods. For this reason, sometimes salt is used more than once in a recipe.

smoking: A gentle way of cooking food by applying indirect heat — smoke — which also adds flavour. It is also used to preserve food.

temperature, controlling: Adjusting temperatures is the most common way to control the different levels of cooking for one ingredient, for example a hot sear to cook the exterior of a whole eye fillet, followed by a slower cook at a lower temperature to cook the interior, while carefully adding ice to a cooking pot will instantly cool the temperature and arrest the cooking process.

time, allowing for: Allowing sufficient time for the magic to happen after the action has been initiated lies behind much of the alchemy of cooking.

yeast, activating: Adding sugar will activate yeast, causing it to form bubbles which will aerate a mixture.

WEIGHTS, MEASURES *and* TEMPERATURES

This book provides both metric and imperial measures, and temperatures in Celsius and Fahrenheit. The conversions are generally rounded up or down, and any small variations won't impact on the results.

Unless otherwise noted:

for larger amounts: Cups are generally used for dry and liquid ingredients (e.g., flour, sugar, water). For the recipes in this book, it is not necessary to differentiate between a metric cup and US standard cups.

for smaller amounts: Teaspoons and tablespoons are used, where possible. Here again there is a small variation in their volume around the world.

for recipes where a more precise measure is needed: For liquid ingredients, millilitres and fluid ounces are provided, and occasionally pints and litres. For dry ingredients, grams and ounces are provided. Conversions are approximate, rounded up or down to the nearest practical amount.

OVENS

Where ovens are used, the recipes assume a fan-forced oven. If you don't have one, you'll just need to increase the temperature by 10 degrees or so, or cook for a little longer. There are always variations in the way ovens perform, so observe the food as it cooks and let your senses – sight, taste, touch, smell, sound — be your guide. With experience comes intuition, the 'sixth sense', and that can be the most useful guide of all.

MISE EN PLACE . . . OR NOT

It's usual for cooks and chefs to assemble the ingredients before commencing a cook, and the ingredients list is for that purpose. Many of those lists go further and include some preparation: 'onions, sliced', 'garlic, crushed', 'freshly-ground pepper', 'ginger, grated' and so on. That works well in high-volume hospitality settings, but the downside is a significant element of freshness can be lost. Some chopped ingredients can sit around for a while and won't lose too much of their flavours, texture, and aromas, but others will suffer and the dish will be compromised. There is no comparison, for example, between parsley that has been freshly picked and then sliced just before use and parsley that has been left for some time to wilt in a bowl; pepper may stay hot but will lose its high notes soon after being ground.

Too much focus on mise en place can become formulaic and also take away from intuition, creativity, and the theatre of the cook: reaching for what is needed; chopping, slicing and crushing as food sizzles in the pan; and reaching for more if the first grab wasn't quite enough. So, in this book the ingredients list usually includes only the most preliminary of steps, such as peeling. Chopping, slicing, crushing, and squeezing is left to the method. Occasional exceptions are made when it would be too awkward to do those things while cooking because the chef or cook's hands are otherwise tied.

SERVING SIZES

Serving sizes are not included because they are too variable and not applicable in many circumstances: people, for example, will put as many or as few steaks on the barbecue as they want to serve. In general terms, and unless otherwise stated, the recipes are suitable for 3-4 serves.

RECIPES

Always read the recipe through before starting, to make sure you have all the ingredients, and also to visualize the steps. That helps ensure you have allowed enough time, and will also help you to coordinate the various steps of the more detailed recipes.

INGREDIENTS

High-quality ingredients always give the best results. Fresh is generally best, although sometimes frozen or dried may also be needed. Vegetables and fruit might keep for a while, but as soon as they are picked — and therefore removed from their own source of nutrition — they begin to deteriorate, even if slowly.

Note also that:

olive oil: Extra virgin olive oil (EVOO) is the best choice, but if none is to hand standard olive oil will work almost as well and is fine for frying. Don't substitute other oils when the recipe calls for olive oil.

neutral oil: This refers to oils that are relatively flavourless so won't affect the flavour of the other ingredients. They are generally used for frying and baking and have high smoke points, meaning they can reach a high temperature without burning. Good ones to use are vegetable, canola, and grapeseed oils.

butter: Salted butter is used, unless otherwise stated

STORING FOODS

Most prepared meals should be kept in the fridge, covered or in an air-tight container, and consumed within a few days of preparation.

Some exceptions include Steak Tartare, which cannot be stored and must be eaten very soon after being made and, on the other hand, condiments and preserves, which if sealed correctly will keep for longer, but then usually should be eaten within a few days of opening. Condiments with a high acid and sugar content do however keep for longer.

With all foods, follow usual hygiene and storage instructions and watch for signs of spoilage: strange or unpleasant odours, discolourations, changes in texture, mould growth and so on. If in doubt, throw it out.

OUTDOOR COOKING

Many of the recipes are well-suited to cooking outdoors, on a barbecue, in a wood oven, or even over a firepit (campfire)

If this outdoor equipment isn't available, the recipes can still be cooked on a stovetop or in a conventional oven.

Cooking over a barbecue or firepit (campfire)

This normally entails sizzling the foods on a grill plate (griddle). Any type of barbecue is suitable: electric, gas, or wood, all of which will heat the grill plate in readiness for cooking.

If cooking over a firepit, the main principle is to build up a good fire under the plate and then allow it to die down to hot embers that will become covered with a layer of ash but still be red hot within. By this time, the grill plate should be at a good temperature for cooking.

Cooking in this way rarely entails having the food in direct contact with the flame although a South American cooking method known as 'rescoldo' requires burying the food in the hot ashes.

Whether cooking on a barbecue or firepit, ideally it should have two heat zones: a high-heat zone for searing, and then a lower-heat zone for more gentle cooking. Controlling the heat on the plate is usually a matter of having a higher number of hot coals under the hot zone and a lesser number under the lower-heat zone. Moving the coals around as needed will help control the heat while 'on the go'.

Sometimes, if the plate becomes too hot, a quick wipe with a damp tea-towel — wearing heatproof gloves — will help lower the temperature.

Some foods need to be cooked slowly and may need to be elevated on a rack well above the flame, such as when cooking a whole tenderloin (eye fillet). As a large piece of meat, there is a risk of burning it on the outside and under-cooking it on the inside if it is left on high heat for too long. Instead, it would normally be initially seared on the hot plate, left to cook a little longer, and then moved to the high rack for the final stages. In any case, elevating the food above the heat source will also effectively moderate the heat.

facing page: *in Patagonia, preparing to cook a carcass of lamb over a firepit in the traditional 'Asado' manner, where the carcass is held in a cage-like grill called a 'parrilla' and then cooked very slowly, for seven hours or more, over the flames, and basted all the while with 'salmuera' (a mix of heavily salted water and aromatics).*

Judging the temperature

Most barbecues come with a built-in thermometer, or you can use an infrared one — or even the 'hand test': just hold your hand, palm facing down, about 7 cm / 3 in. above the grill plate. Count the seconds until you have to remove your hand because of the heat. If you can only count up to 1–2 seconds before taking your hand away, the plate is very hot; for 3–4 seconds, it is hot; and for 5 seconds it is a medium heat.

Guidelines for when cooking over a firepit

This always takes place outside, which means there are external factors that will impact on the cooking over which you have little control. There are some basic rules:

1. **Safety first** — have a bucket or two of water close-by, as well as a fire blanket or a shovel and some dirt with which to smother the fire if necessary.

2. **Use proper equipment** — heat-proof cooking gloves and utensils, including forks, tongs, scrapers, and prongs, as well as chopping boards and sharp knives.

3. **Have sanitiser and paper towels** — to deal with all the wiping and handling.

4. **Keep foods separate** — don't put raw and cooked foods on the same plate. Also keep chopping boards and utensils clean.

5. **Pick the location carefully** — a sheltered spot is needed, one that is away from winds that might stir up and spread embers, but which is also well clear of any buildings, overhanging branches, and of course flammable materials.

6. **Contain the fire** — keep it within a fire-proof boundary, something as simple as a ring of stones but more ideally a cast-iron ring that will reflect some heat and therefore help the cooking process. Some people build their fire in a pit.

7. **Keep the fire at a manageable size** — this is a size that you can quickly extinguish on your own if there is a sudden and unexpected turn of events.

8. **Fully extinguish** — when you have finished cooking, douse the fire with water and stir it through the embers to put out the fire completely.

9. **Watch the weather** — windy days are not suitable for outdoor cooking. Mild breezes shouldn't pose a problem, but the fire should be upstream from them, so smoke blows away, not over the food (or you). Very hot or rainy days are not suitable for fire cooking either. It is something that is best enjoyed in milder weather.

Cooking in a wood-fired oven

Variations of these domed outdoor ovens are found around the globe. Often called 'pizza ovens', in Italy such an oven is known as a 'forno a legna per pizza' (wood-fired oven for pizza), and as a 'horno de barro' (clay oven) in Spain and South America. The most important detail is to build a powerful fire within and allow it plenty of time, usually at least 3 hours, to fully heat up. Always follow the manufacturer's instructions.

above: *Simon's wood-fired oven, backyard, Taralga*

Smokers

Another great piece of outdoor equipment is a smoker, where smoke from burning woodchips (kept at a distance) gently cooks the food. The woodchips are usually flavoured and then impart that flavour to the food. Follow the manufacturer's instructions for your smoker, and note the detail regarding the 'flatline' (see p. 129)

COOKING TEMPERATURES

When cooking meat (all types, including poultry and fish), the internal temperature is important for two reasons: first, safety, and second, flavour and texture.

Safety

With rare exception, meat must be cooked to a minimum temperature before taken off the heat. Some will be ready to eat immediately, while others must be rested for a few minutes, during which time the internal temperature will continue to rise, after which they will be safe for consumption. (Rare exceptions include Steak Tartare, Carpaccio, and Sushi, all of which have specific instructions to offset any food-safety risks).

Recommended temperatures for cooked meats in this book are provided below, as set by the US Department of Agriculture (USDA). in practice, however, many people prefer whole cuts of red meats, steak in particular, to be cooked to lower temperatures. These fresh cuts would not normally have contaminants internally but it is most important to sear and brown the meat all over, to destroy any contaminants on the surface. People will then, generally, cook the meat to suit their taste, but it should be noted that there is an increased risk of contamination at the lower internal temperatures.

Flavour and texture

Once safety considerations have been dealt with, temperature and its impact on flavour and texture comes into play, especially where red meats — beef, pork, lamb — are concerned. Although most chefs would agree these meats are at their best when served after the minimal amount of cooking, some people prefer them to be cooked for longer, and this is a matter of personal taste.

The detail is that the cooking process breaks down the connective tissue in the meat and it becomes juicy and tender as gelatin is formed. If over-cooked, however, the muscle fibres shrink and meat loses too much moisture, so it becomes tough and dry. 'Medium' is the popular option that sits in the middle: neither too bloody nor too dry.

Gauging the 'doneness' of red meat

This becomes easier with experience. How the meat looks on the inside is the most accurate guide — the colour will range from bloody red through to grey as it passes through the stages of raw through to well-done. The level of 'pinkness' indicates where it sits in the popular medium–rare through to medium–well (or well-done) range. But it's not ideal to cut through meat to check doneness, especially while still cooking, as that will release juices and therefore moisture. It also doesn't allow for the on-going cooking that takes place after the meat has been removed from the heat. The visual appearance can also be misleading as those juices can make it appear more rare than it actually is. The other option is to cut into it after it is plated, but that is awkward when serving (especially if it needs to be taken back to the heat) — and it is just too late.

'Feel' therefore becomes the more useful approach. Steaks will feel soft and fleshy, as they are, when they are raw, less so as they cook. To test this, some people spread apart their forefinger and thumb and then bring them closer together in 5 steps. They then pinch the soft, loose flesh in between and compare that to the feel of the meat. If they feel about the same at the widest point between finger and thumb, the meat is rare, and at the closest point well-done, with the various other stages lying in between.

This itself can be confusing, unfortunately. 'Feel' can be imagined, though. Some chefs and cooks gauge doneness more intuitively: they feel the steak and then imagine how it would feel if they were biting into it, while also considering how it looks (externally) and its aroma. Checking the temperature is the other option, but there is considerable variation in guidelines provided by different sources which just adds to confusion.

Product	Minimum internal temperature & rest time
Beef, pork, and lamb steaks, chops, roasts[1]	63°C / 145°F, then allow to rest for at least 3 minutes during which time the temperature will rise further
All poultry	74°C / 165°F
Eggs	71°C / 160°F
Fish & Shellfish	63°C / 145°F

Source: USDA Food Safety & Inspection Service; temperatures rounded to nearest whole number

1. Excludes roasts with stuffing. Higher internal temperature of 75°C / 167°F are recommended for meats that have been processed included stuffed, rolled, boned, minced or mechanically tenderized products.

following pages: Misty dawn at Gostwyck, New South Wales

Vegetables | Salads

PEAR, WALNUT *and* BLUE CHEESE SALAD

preparation: *10 minutes or thereabouts*

½ cup walnuts

1 pear

2 cups soft lettuce leaves

90 g / 3 oz blue cheese, or to taste

¼ cup olive oil

3 tbsp white wine vinegar, or to taste

1 tsp honey, optional

1 tsp dijon mustard

salt & pepper, to taste

THIS SIMPLE, VERSATILE SALAD is made from young lettuce leaves, thin slices of pear, crushed roasted walnuts and morsels of creamy blue cheese, all gently tossed together in a light vinaigrette.

It is important to use a lettuce with a soft rather than crispier leaf as that works best with the crunch of the walnuts, the juiciness of the pear, and the creaminess of the cheese. I like to use butter lettuce, and mignonette also works well.

This is a lovely salad to pair with any grilled meat and I often serve it alongside a scotch fillet, together with a creamy mushroom sauce (see p. 118 for the Scotch Fillet and Creamy Mushroom Sauce recipe).

METHOD: First chop the walnuts into nibble-sized chunks then quickly toast them. This is best done in the oven for an even result (see p. 86 for notes on toasting pine nuts: follow the same method although the walnuts might take a little longer).

If you are pressed for time, you can of course toast them in a hot, dry pan. Always watch them, as nuts and seeds burn very quickly.

Either way, once they are nicely toasted, put them to one side and allow them to cool.

Rinse the pear but don't peel it. Use a mandolin or a very sharp knife to slice it very finely into moist, translucent pieces while discarding the seeds and core. Then break the blue cheese into small bite-sized pieces. A little bit of more crumbled cheese in the mix also works well.

Finally, remove the larger outer leaves from the lettuce, then rinse and drain the remaining leaves.

Dry with paper towels or spin in a lettuce spinner. Toss all the salad ingredients together in a bowl, adding the cheese last so it does not break up too much.

The dressing is very simple and can be modified further to taste. Just before serving the salad, place all the oil, vinegar, honey (if using), dijon mustard, and seasonings in a lidded jar. Give it a good shake for about a minute to emulsify, then pour over the salad, just before serving.

above: *Pear, Walnut and Blue Cheese Salad*

HEIRLOOM TOMATO SALAD

preparation: *about 15 minutes*

2–3 heirloom tomatoes

for the dressing:

bunch of fresh dill

100 ml / 3 fl. oz maple syrup

100 ml / 3 fl. oz white wine vinegar

4–5 tbsp dijon mustard, to taste

1 cup grapeseed oil

salt & pepper, to season

to serve:

sprouts, fresh herbs, edible flowers, etc., to garnish

goats or bocconcini cheese

toasted pine nuts, optional

HEIRLOOM TOMATOES provide a deeper and more authentic tomato flavour, one that is generally earthy and sweet, than the more readily available hybrid varieties. They are naturally pollinated and true to seed (meaning the offspring will grow to be the same as the parent plant), and traditionally their seeds have been passed down through families over many generations. They come in a lovely array of shapes, colours and sizes, are often pleated (which makes for very decorative slices), and all in all provide an aesthetic and tasty experience. On the downside, they are more expensive and vulnerable to disease than hybrids, are only seasonally available, and they won't keep on the shelf for very long.

This recipe makes quite a lot of dressing, more than is needed for one sitting, but it will keep in the fridge for at least 3 months. Otherwise, you can easily scale back the quantity of each ingredient to produce a lesser amount.

METHOD: Using a stick blender, take a few moments to blend all of the dressing ingredients except for the oil. Once that is done, drizzle in the oil in a steady stream as you continue to blend. The dressing will soon begin to emulsify, but if you are looking for a thicker consistency you can add in a little more oil as needed. Season to taste.

Pour the desired amount of dressing into a salad bowl. Dice tomatoes into uneven chunks and toss through the dressing. Garnish with sprouts or fresh herbs (such as chervil, watercress) and serve with goats or bocconcini cheese. Toasted pine nuts (see p. 86) are also a tasty addition.

facing page: *Heirloom Tomato Salad*

BAKED ASPARAGUS *with* SOUS VIDE EGG

preparation and cooking : *a little over an hour, approx.*

2 eggs per serve

1-2 bunches asparagus, or as needed

2-3 tbsp olive oil, approx.

a sprinkle of salt flakes

some freshly-ground pepper

1 slice sourdough bread per serve

squeeze of fresh lemon juice, optional

enough butter to spread on the bread

Suggested accompaniments:

wilted spinach or chard

rocket

finely sliced spring onion

goats curd

freshly grated parmesan

fresh mint

lemon zest and / or juice

horseradish

IF YOU'RE LUCKY ENOUGH TO have a sous vide, these eggs are one of the best things for which it can be used. The egg yolks begin to cook at around 65°C / 149°F, so the sous vide temperature should be set just a little lower, to 64°C / 147°F. To achieve a slightly cooked, oozy yolk, the eggs are left in at that temperature in the sous vide for around an hour (to ensure they are safe to eat). They then become a great addition to ramen soup or, as in this case, can be used as a kind of sauce to be served alongside baked asparagus or other greens. Depending on how you like the texture of your egg, you can reduce the sous vide temperature slightly, to 63°C / 145°F — which is why recipes that cook eggs in this way are often known as '63°C Eggs'.

METHOD: Set the sous vide to the desired temperature, as described above and, once that is reached, lower in the whole eggs (still in their shells). Allow them an hour to cook (it won't matter if you go a little over that time — they won't overcook — but don't go under it).

Meanwhile, heat your oven to 200°C / 390°F. As it heats up, give the asparagus a quick rinse and remove the woody ends. The easiest way is to just bend each asparagus until it snaps: that will happen at exactly the right place on the stalk, just where the stem begins to get tough.

Place the olive oil along with the salt and some freshly ground pepper in a shallow baking tray. Toss through the asparagus so they are well covered in the oil, and then spread them out in a single layer in the tray. Bake in the oven for about 10–15 minutes (depending on their size — pencil-thin asparagus will cook quickly, while the thicker ones will of course take longer). To check whether the asparagus is cooked, spear one with a fork: it should pass through the asparagus without resistance. The asparagus by this time will have darkened slightly in colour, while their undersides should be slightly browned and their tips still green. They should be ready to serve at the same time as the sous vide eggs but, as noted earlier, you can leave the eggs to sit in the sous vide for a little while longer if you need to give the asparagus some extra baking time.

Another lovely way to prepare the asparagus is to cook them in a heavy-based pan over an open fire (see below). Just toss them through the oil and season them, then turn them gently with tongs as they cook (they won't take long, but it will depend on the size). Don't burn them, but it won't matter if they become slightly charred; it will add another flavour dimension. You can also add a small amount of lemon juice just as you are about to serve. Don't add the lemon juice while cooking as it tends to become bitter.

A minute or so before you are ready to take the asparagus from the oven, pop some thick slices of sourdough bread in a toaster or grill. Once they are nicely toasted, spread generously with butter. Moving quickly so everything stays hot, use a slotted spoon to remove the eggs from the sous vide, crack open their shells, and gently slide the egg over the buttered toast. The egg (white and yolk) should remain intact, but the yolk will be runny when the egg is cut open. Serve alongside the asparagus, topped with your preferred accompaniments.

above: *asparagus cooking over an open fire*

BART'S PEPPERS

preparation and cooking : *30–40 minutes*

6–7 capsicums, assorted colours

150 ml / 5 fl.oz olive oil

2–4 tbsp balsamic vinegar

1 tbsp honey

5–6 garlic cloves, peeled

thyme leaves, optional

salt flakes, to season

freshly ground paper, to season

BART BORGHESI, my grandfather, most likely learnt how to prepare capsicums in this way from his own father Nello, who emigrated from Italy in the early 20th century. Travelling by ship with little more than a ravioli roller upon which to build a new life, he would go on to become largely responsible for introducing fine pasta, in particular ravioli, to the Anglo-Australian community of Melbourne.[1] In those days, their palates were not accustomed to such foods and the challenges were great, a far cry from the pasta-devouring hordes of today — yet Nello would establish many restaurants and cafés, working on his own and also with notable Italian chefs, hotels and restaurants, always supported and partnered by his wife Bruna. He also founded the La Tosca pasta factory, named for the Puccini opera *La Tosca*. It was both an acknowledgement of his great love of opera and also the detail that he and Puccini shared the same birth place of Lucca, in Tuscany.

Bart always emphasised the importance of choosing capsicums with thick flesh — otherwise the charred skins would peel off in scraps, leaving little 'meat' to eat and a soggy mess on the bench. Equally important was the steaming of the charred capsicums. My own father, Gerrard, remembers Bart carefully charring the capsicums over his hand-built wood barbecue in suburban Hawthorn back in the 1960s, before wrapping them in newspaper so they could steam up —

facing page : *roasting peppers and onions in the hot coals*

---

1. 'La Tosca Food Processing Company, Melbourne', Museums Victoria, https://collections.museumsvictoria.com.au/articles/1646

above: *peeling and de-seeding, and the finished dish*

and the inevitable cursing that followed should the flesh then prove to be too thin or the capsicums bitter and stringy. Plump, sweet, richly coloured capsicums with smoky notes and dressed with a glistening blot of golden olive oil was the desired result. Even then, olive oil was hard to come by in the suburbs of Melbourne, and Bart would become particularly excited when one of his cousins, who travelled to Italy quite frequently, returned with large gallon-sized tins of this precious commodity.

Bart also preferred to use red capsicums but sometimes used green as they were cheaper, although slightly bitter rather than sweet. I like to use a mix — red, orange and yellow, for the vibrancy of colour and the sweet flavours — but some green ones can also be mixed in for both the colour and earthy flavour contrasts they provide.

METHOD: This is a great thing to do when starting a fire that will later be used for cooking. I like to, very carefully (using tongs), sit the capsicum directly on the fire so that the initial stages of flames and heat can blister the skin heavily without needing to overcook the capsicum. It is sometimes said that the vegetables (and other foods) should never come in direct contact with flame, but I make an exception with this kind of charring that only effects the skins and is important to the flavour of the dish. It only takes a few minutes. You want a completely charred outside and for the shape of the capsicum to be just beginning to wilt, a sign that it has just lost its structure but hasn't disintegrated entirely.

Next, using tongs and gloves, remove the capsicums from the fire and wrap them individually in sheets of newspaper, then sit them in a bowl to rest for about 15 minutes. Alternatively, if you are worried about smudging ink, you can place them in a bowl and cover with kitchen film, although this takes something away from the woody earthiness that the newspaper seems to impart.

Meanwhile, finely chop or crush the garlic. Mix together with all the remaining ingredients and allow the flavours to meld as the capsicums continue to rest. After enough time has passed, unwrap each capsicum and use the back of a knife to peel or scrape off the charred skin. If the capsicums were properly charred and had nice, plump flesh, it should come off cleanly and easily. Slice the flesh into strips and place in a dish with the prepared marinade of all the other ingredients. Serve as an accompaniment to barbecued or grilled meats, or in an antipasto or spread over crunchy bread.

COAL-ROASTED ONIONS

preparation & cooking: *about 1 hour*

5–6 large white onions

olive oil, to dress

sherry vinegar, optional

salt & pepper, to season

A DELICIOUS WAY TO COOK ONIONS is to simply place them whole and unpeeled directly amongst the hot coals of a campfire, firepit, or barbecue (using heatproof gloves, of course). Keeping them in their skins retains all the moisture and flavour and allows them to gently steam in their husks.

Shallots (or 'french shallots', see p. 102) can be used in place of onions, although they will take much less time to cook. It is best to use larger ones with several layers of skin, as the small ones with more delicate skins will too easily dry out.

Shallots can be quite sweet, and so it is okay to leave the roots attached before roasting (provided any dirt is rinsed off beforehand), because this will help produce some dark, concentrated, and usually chewy caramelization at the vegetable's base, just inside the skin. This contrasts nicely to the smooth, roasted flesh and also gives an attractive, rustic appearance to the dish.

It is not unusual, in relaxed settings, for people to hold the whole roasted shallot by the roots and base, and then use their teeth to pull and scrape off the flesh — a bit like scraping the flesh off an artichoke except that all layers of flesh, other than perhaps the most outermost ones, are eaten. Serviettes are essential . . .

The right time to roast the onions (or shallots) is when the coals are at ember stage and covered in a fine layer of ash but still red-hot within. Spread the vegetables out throughout the coals so they are not touching each

facing page: *selecting onions and beetroots to roast in the hot coals*

other, and then partially bury them. Turn them occasionally to completely and evenly char their outsides, until they begin to feel soft (depending on the heat and size of the onions or shallots, this usually takes between 20 and 30 minutes). You can use a gloved hand to gently squeeze them around their roundest part to check their softness (and the more you practise this, the better judge you will be) or, if you prefer, insert a skewer at about the 15-minute mark (a little earlier for shallots). It should glide in and out easily, with minimal or no resistance; otherwise, continue cooking for a few more minutes, as required. Resist the urge to skewer too early, as a hole in the skin will compromise the build-up of steam and therefore interfere with the cooking process.

When they are soft enough, remove them from the coals and allow them to cool for about 5–10 minutes, during which time they will continue to cook and soften further. Once cool enough to handle, remove the skins and, if you have retained the roots at the base, carefully sponge off any ash (a clean tea-towel, wetted with hot water, works well), and then fluff the dampened roots out again with your fingers. The roots themselves are not eaten, and the heat of the coals would, in any case, have killed any lingering bacteria, but still they need to be clean.

Cut the peeled and roasted onions into thick long slices. Shallots can usually just be quartered of halved, and occasionally, if they are not too large, left whole. Dress with olive oil and season with salt before serving, and brighten them up with a splash of sherry vinegar if desired.

Fire-roasted vegetables make a lovely accompaniment to any meal and are best served when they are still warm. They can also be used, when cooled, in antipasto, but generally they are not suitable for storing and should be eaten within 24 hours of cooking.

facing page: *peeled and seasoned coal-roasted onions*
above: *peeling the charred onions*

CONFIT GARLIC

preparation & cooking: *about 1 hour*

several garlic cloves, peeled

vegetable or grapeseed oil, to cover

salt flakes, to season

THIS IS AN EASILY MADE, versatile condiment, essentially garlic cloves poached very slowly in olive oil. It is lovely as a simple spread on bread, but it is also used to enrich the flavour of sauces, baked dishes, pizzas, stuffings and more. It can even be added to salad dressings.

I usually make it using 12 or so medium-sized cloves which I then simmer in about a third of a cup of olive oil, but you can make as little or as much as you like. The ratio of oil-to-cloves will vary, depending on the diameter of your pot. They must be fully submerged in the oil; the heat must be very low; and the cooking time very, very slow.

METHOD: Place the cloves in a pot and cover with the oil. Allow them to cook over a very low heat, so they are barely simmering. Some people cook them in a low oven, but I prefer the stovetop approach, because then I can more easily keep an eye on them and make sure they don't get too hot. Either way is fine.

After an hour or so, the garlic should be soft and gently golden and very fragrant. Drain off any excess oil and season the garlic with salt flakes. You should be able to lift the softened cloves with a butter knife or similar and spread the garlic directly onto bread or another base, without any additional processing.

Alternatively, you can lightly mash the cloves with a spoon or fork, to form a paste. Confit garlic should be served soon after making, with any left-overs kept, covered, in the fridge and used within a few days.

facing page: *garlic cooking in oil*

above: *beetroot roasting in the hot ashes*

BEETROOT RESCOLDO

preparation & cooking : *1–2 hours*

a bunch or more of fresh beetroot

coarse or flaked salt

Cooking with ash

This popular outdoor method is used in Argentina and other South American countries. It provides a unique way to enjoy the natural flavour of various ingredients while adding a delicious smoky twist. Beyond that, historically it led to the development of 'nixtamalization', a process whereby corn (maize) kernels are cooked in a mixture of water and ash, or other substances such as lime. Through a series of reactions, this enables the bound niacin in the corn to be released and to become nutritionally available, an important detail given niacin deficiency is a cause of potentially fatal diseases such as pellagra.

ALSO KNOWN AS 'Remolachas al Rescoldo' in Spanish, this traditional Argentinian dish is made by cooking the beets in the residual heat of a bonfire or hot ashes, which imparts a smoky flavour and enhances their natural sweetness.

METHOD: Begin by starting a fire and letting it burn until the flames have died down and you have a good bed of hot embers and ashes.

Meanwhile, cut off the stems and quickly rinse off any excess dirt. then individually wrap each beet in foil. In Chile, we used to place them, skins on, directly in the hot ash and leave them overnight, but this can overcook them.

Make sure you wrap each one up tightly to prevent any ashes from getting inside, then carefully bury them in the hot ashes. Cover them fully with ash, and then leave them for 1–2 hours.

To check if they are ready, carefully remove one from the ashes using tongs or a long stick. Open the foil and pierce the beet with a fork or knife. If it goes through easily, its ready. If not, wrap it up again and bury for a little longer.

Once all the beets are cooked, carefully remove them from the ashes using tongs or a shovel. Unwrap and allow them to cool for a few minutes, then peel them using your hands or a knife.

Slice them into rounds or chunks and then sprinkle the salt over the top. Enjoy this rustic dish as a smoky, flavoursome accompaniment to grilled meats or as part of a picnic spread.

CRUSHED POTATOES

preparation & cooking : *about 1 hour*

several small-medium all-purpose potatoes

clarified butter

salt flakes, to season

to clarify butter

Gently melt some unsalted butter in a bowl over simmering water. Don't stir; just allow it to split into three layers: a base of water and milk solids; a thin layer of foam on top; and in between a thick layer of golden butterfat (the clarified butter). To separate it from the other layers, skim off the foam layer using a wide, shallow spoon then slowly pour the butterfat into another container, tipping the pot at a minimal angle, to allow only the butterfat to decant, while the milk solids and water remain in the pot. If any more foam begins to form on top of the butterfat after decanting, remove by straining the butterfat through cheesecloth or a fine mesh sieve.

EVERYONE LOVES THESE crushed, buttery, fried potatoes, and I usually make several batches. It's important to use all-purpose, quite floury potatoes (e.g., coliban, pontiac, sabago, désirée) and lots of butter: the usual ratio is about 10:1 or, in other words, 10 times as much potato in weight to butter (e.g., 100 g of butter per kg of potatoes or about 1½ oz butter for 1 lb potatoes) . . . but you won't be alone if you add some extra clarified butter.

How much you can make will also be ruled by the size of your pan. There should only be one layer of potatoes frying at a time, and they should not be touching each other: as always, it's important not to crowd the pan.

So, first you'll need to work out how many slightly squashed, boiled potatoes will fit comfortably in the pan and then work out how much butter you'll need. This doesn't need to be exact: just enough to ensure the potatoes can bubble away comfortably in the butter as they form a lovely golden crust.

Clarified butter is needed because it can be heated to a high temperature without burning. It is simply unsalted butter with the milk solids and water removed. If making your own, about 25% of the original volume will be lost during this process, so you should start with 25% more butter than what you'll eventually use. It is so easy to make that it's best done as needed, although it will keep in a sealed jar at room temperature for a few weeks, and longer in the fridge or freezer (provided no water or contaminants are introduced as they will cause it to spoil).

facing page : *getting ready to flatten the potatoes in the back garden at Taralga*

METHOD: First work out how much clarified butter you will need to fry the potatoes (using the 1 : 10 ratio as a guide) and have a little extra in case it is needed.

Bring a pot of well-salted water to the boil. Add the potatoes and then reduce to a brisk simmer. Cook the potatoes for 15–20 minutes, or until they are just tender enough to squash in a tea towel into slightly flattened discs, without falling apart.

Melt a generous amount of clarified butter in a heavy-based pan then add the potato discs, just enough to sit in the pan without crowding. How much butter to use depends on how much potato you can fit in the pan, but obviously if you are using half of the potatoes in your first batch of frying, you would also use half the total amount of prepared butter. It doesn't need to be too exact.

Gently fry the potatoes over a medium-high heat for 20-30 minutes, until a golden crust develops on the bases. You may need to increase the heat slightly if the crust is taking too long to form, and add more butter if the pan is drying out. Once the crusts have formed, flip the potatoes and sprinkle over with flaked salt to draw out the moisture. Add some more butter as needed, and cook for another 20 minutes or so until a golden crust has formed on the other side. Flip the potatoes once more, sprinkle salt over the newly crusted bases, and serve immediately. The potatoes should have a crisp outer shell and be fluffy on the inside.

They can also be cooked on a barbecue plate or in a hot oven in a shallow baking tray, turned and salted in the same manner as above, until crisp and golden.

facing page: *flattened potatoes baking in clarified butter*
above: *flattening the potatoes before baking*

EGGPLANT ESCABECHE

preparation & cooking : *about 30 minutes*

2–3 small–medium eggplants

1 cup white wine vinegar

1 cup water

1 tbsp peppercorns

1 bay leaf

200 ml / 7 fl. oz olive oil

2 tsp neutral oil

1 tsp dried oregano

1 tsp dried chilli

black pepper, to taste

garlic, to taste

facing page: *pumpkin, squash, zucchini, onions, peppers, eggplant, and garlic are all suitable for roasting over hot coals. Just toss in olive oil then season and bake over the coals covered with foil. Once cooked, they will be soft with some caramelization, and the sweet flavours will have melded deliciously with the olive oil, like a fire-baked ratatouille. Potatoes are less suitable to use as they take longer to cook and lack the sweetness of the other vegetables.*

'ESCABECHE' IS THE SPANISH TERM for pickling, and this method is used throughout Argentina and other parts of South America. It is a great way to preserve eggplant.

When selecting an eggplant, first take note of the 'dimple' at its base. If it is small and round, the eggplant will contain less seeds than those with more of an oval slit at the base. It is a common myth that this denotes the sex of the fruit, when in fact eggplant fruits contain both male and female parts. Eggplants with fewer seeds are, however, more suitable for pickling and cooking generally, as the seeds can make them bitter. Generally, the eggplant should feel quite firm and dense and have a glossy, deep purple, unbruised or marked skin.

For this dish, whether to leave the skin on or off is optional: some prefer the additional texture provided by the skin, while others enjoy the softened flesh of peeled eggplants. I like the happy medium — leaving half of the skin of the eggplant on and removing the rest. It seems to give the most interesting result.

Eggplant Escabeche can make an appearance practically anywhere on the dinner table, but goes especially well with meats, bread, cheeses and salads.

METHOD: Slice the eggplant downwards into chunky finger-sized batons. Place in a colander and salt generously then leave for 20 minutes, tossing every once in a while.

Meanwhile, prepare the vinegar and oil mixtures, as follows:

for the vinegar mixture: This is made of equal parts vinegar and water, plus aromatics, and you will need enough liquid to cover the eggplant completely. That will depend on the size of the eggplants and also the size of your pot. A cup of each is usually enough, but if not just add some more water and vinegar, in equal amounts.

Add the peppercorns and the bay leaf and bring to the boil. This will produce pungent vapours, so make sure the cooking vents are open, or open a window.

Blanch in a heavy boil, and then rinse the sliced eggplant in cold water and add it to the pot. Allow it to cook for 3–4 minutes, until it has begun to soften but is still holding its shape. It should be cooked, but still slightly firm or spongy. Be careful not to cook it for too long, as that will cause it to break down too much.

Strain the eggplant, but reserve the vinegar liquid as it will be added back to the mix to achieve the right acidity.

for the oil mixture: Separately, to make the escabeche liquid, mix together the olive oil and a good dash of the neutral oil (which will stop the olive oil from congealing at lower temperatures).

Add the dried oregano, dried chilli and black pepper.

Next, add back some of the reserved vinegar (from cooking the eggplant) and then taste. Start with about 1 teaspoon (about half the amount of neutral oil used), then taste again, and add more if needed. You are looking for an acidic yet balanced marinade for the eggplant. If it isn't acidic enough, it will not keep as well out of the fridge. You will also need enough escabeche to fill your pickling jars.

to store: Fill sterilised glass jars with the eggplant. Cover with the hot vinegar marinade and fill the jars right to the top then seal. Allow to cool in the fridge, after which the jars can be stored on a pantry shelf.

If properly sealed, the escabeche will keep on the shelf for 3–6 months, but once opened should be refrigerated and used within a few days.

When serving, add some freshly minced garlic, to taste. Traditionally, this was included in the vinegar marinade, but health authorities now generally advise against storing mixes of garlic and oil for lengthy periods.

GOCHUJANG EGGPLANT

preparation & cooking: *about 15 minutes*

2 large eggplants

1–2 tbsp olive oil

2 tbsp gochujang paste

1 tbsp water

GOCHUJUNG IS A FERMENTED KOREAN condiment, deep red in colour and with a distinctive flavour that is pungent, smoky, spicy, and sweet. It gains its rich colour from red peppers, which are mixed with sticky rice, soy beans, aromatics, sweeteners, and seasonings to form a paste.

Gochujang paste can be made at home — recipes are easily found — but it takes considerable effort and time. On the other hand, bought varieties, readily available at Asian groceries and some supermarkets, provide an excellent, fast result. In my view, it is the selection of eggplants (see p. 51) and care in the cooking process that lifts the flavours of this dish, rather than the source of the gochujang.

Grilling the eggplants rather than frying them means they will not soak up too much oil.

This is my favourite way to serve eggplant, delicious in a ramen, as an accompaniment to meat, or as part of a warm salad. It will keep, covered, in the fridge for a day or two — probably even longer — but its flavour is at its most piquant and fresh if served hot and freshly made.

METHOD: Pre-heat your grill / broiler to a medium-high heat and your oven to 200°C / 390°F.

Next, slice the eggplants into finger-thick batons and brush each face generously and evenly with oil. There is no need to salt the eggplants first.

Grill until the eggplant has developed some deeper colour on one side (not too much), and then turn them over. Continue grilling until the eggplant is soft but not fully cooked all the way through, because they are still to go in the oven. Ideally, it should be soft on the outside but firm enough on the inside to hold its shape. In this way, its texture is very different to the soft, sautéed and usually quite oily eggplant often used in Mediterranean cuisine. All up, the grilling process should take about 6–8 minutes, or 3–4 on each side.

While the eggplant is grilling, mix the gochujang and water together in a bowl.

Once a nice colour has been achieved, brush the tops with the gochujang mixture and place in the hot oven to bake fo 5-10 minutes, or until they are cooked through. Serve immediately.

facing page: *fresh produce at the Rockley market.*
above: *as an alternative to grilling eggplant batons to make Gochujang Eggplant, halved eggplants can be grilled on a large rack over open flames. Oil the surface and season generously with salt, then grill flesh-side down until a nice colour is achieved. Flip them over just for a moment so you can baste the surfaces with the gochujang mixture, then turn them flesh-side down again to finish the cook. The flesh will darken and become sweet and sticky.*

ORANGE, FENNEL *and* RADICCHIO SALAD

preparation: *10 minutes*

½ baby fennel

¼ radicchio (about 1 cup or so)

1 orange

2 tbsp sherry vinegar

4 tbsp olive oil

salt flakes, to season

THIS IS A LIGHT yet deeply flavoured salad that contrasts the sweet notes of orange with heady hints of aniseed and a few bitter nips. The inclusion of fresh orange segments means a burst of fresh juice hits the palate on biting, adding to the dressing and blending the other flavours. Those of orange and fennel are a marriage made in Heaven, and so too are those of orange and duck, so I often serve this salad with Tathra Duck (see p. 89).

METHOD: Peel and segment the orange over a bowl to catch the juice. Place the segments in a salad bowl.

Rinse the fennel and remove any tough outer leaves and cut off the stalks, so you are left with a nice bulb. Slice about half of this finely on a mandolin (the left-over fennel will keep in the fridge for a few days), and then tear up the radicchio.

Toss the sliced fennel and radicchio through the orange segments. Cover the salad and place in the fridge until ready to serve. It should be used on the same day it was prepared.

To make the dressing, place the orange juice, sherry vinegar, and olive oil in a lidded jar, add a pinch of salt flakes, then shake to blend. Taste, and adjust the vinegar, olive oil, and salt as needed, to balance, then toss through the salad just before serving.

facing page: *Orange, Fennel and Radicchio Salad*

SHAKSHUKA

preparation and cooking : *30–40 minutes*

1 red capsicum

1 brown onion, peeled

3 cloves garlic, peeled

2 tomatoes, fresh or tinned

handful of continental parsley

handful of coriander (cilantro)

a few sprigs of dill

2 tsp olive oil

½ tsp smoked paprika

½ tsp cumin

freshly ground pepper, to taste

salt flakes, to taste

100 ml / 3 ½ fl. oz) tomato passata

5 eggs

½ cup greek yoghurt, approx.

THIS SIMPLE BUT FLAVOURSOME meal is made from eggs poached in a fragrant, delicately-spiced tomato sauce and sometimes other vegetables such as capsicum, with cooling yoghurt added to finish. Although it's light, it's also comforting and fulfilling. It is a traditional Northwest African and Middle Eastern dish (from the Magreb), and I first came across it when I was living in the Middle East.

I loved it so much it was, and still is, a favourite breakfast, lunch, or brunch. You will need a wide, lidded frypan to make it.

METHOD: De-seed the capsicum.

Chop the onion and capsicum into small dice, and then finely slice the garlic.

If using fresh tomatoes, peel them by placing them in boiling water for about 30 seconds then rub off the skins.

Rinse the herbs and remove the larger stalks from the parsley, coriander (cilantro), and dill, to leave mostly the leaves. Slice these finely and put to one side.

Place the oil in a wide pan and heat over a moderate heat so it just begins to sizzle. Add the diced vegetables and garlic and then sauté for 5–10 minutes, stirring occasionally, until the onions and capsicums have softened, but not caramelized.

Add the spices. Cook for another minute, and then stir through the diced tomatoes. Continue to cook for a few minutes, until the tomatoes soften and begin to break up.

above: *Shakshuka in the making*

Add the passata, bring to the boil, and then reduce the heat and allow the sauce to simmer over a moderate heat, stirring occasionally, for about 10–15 minutes. It needs to reduce down just enough so that you can part the sauce (the 'Shakshuka') with a spoon to make a clear space for the egg, but it mustn't be dry.

Reduce the heat and, using the spoon, carve 5 small divots into the Shakshuka and break an egg into each one.

Cover the pan with a lid and leave everything to cook on a low temperature for about 3 minutes. Monitor the eggs closely by shaking the pan and 'watching the wobble'. I like to cook mine just until the whites have set but the yolks remain runny. The eggs will continue to cook for a minute or two after you remove them from the heat, so take them off a little earlier than you think, before they are quite ready.

Dollop the yoghurt over the top with a mixture of the freshly chopped herbs, a drizzle of olive oil, and salt flakes. Add some fresh lemon zest if you want, to give the Shakshuka a refreshing zing. Scoop individual serves from the pan and serve with toasted turkish bread.

above: *dipping into the Shakshuka*

ZUCCHINI FRITTERS *with* SMOKED SALMON *and* MARY ROSE

preparation and cooking : *about 50 minutes*

225g / 8oz smoked salmon, approx.

for the Marie Rose sauce:

1 head of garlic

200 g / 7 oz cherry tomatoes

1–2 red chillies, to taste

3–4 tbsp mayonnaise

1 tsp worcestershire sauce

1 tsp maple syrup

lemon wedges to serve

for the fritters:

2 large zucchinis

1 white onion

2 eggs

100 g / 3.5 oz plain / all-purpose flour

1 tsp bicarbonate of soda

pinch of salt

THIS IS A GREAT WAY to use up surplus zucchini when the plants start fruiting heavily in the summer. Be sure to remove most of the excess water by salting them, otherwise, you'll end up with soggy fritters. This is especially important for larger zucchinis, which have a high moisture content.

METHOD: Pre-heat your oven to a very hot 230°C / 445°F. You should get the Marie Rose sauce underway first, as it will take longer to make.

to make the Marie Rose sauce: Split the garlic head in half lengthways and sprinkle the cut side with salt. Wrap it tightly in foil then place on a baking tray with the tomatoes and chilli.

Place them all in the oven for about 20-30 minutes, until their skins just start to blister, but don't let them char.

Remove them from the oven, and then peel and deseed the chillies (it's not necessary to do this for the tomatoes).

Next unwrap the garlic and squeeze the soft cloves out of the skins into a small food processor or hand-held blender, together with the tomatoes and chilli flesh.

Add the remaining ingredients except the lemon, and blitz into a smooth sauce.

to make the fritters: Grate the zucchini coarsely into a colander then sprinkle them with salt and mix well. Leave for about 10 minutes to allow time for the salt to draw out the excess moisture, then use your hands to squeeze them as dry as possible.

Slice up the white onion quite finely and then add it to the zucchini along with the flour, eggs and salt. Mix this thoroughly into a batter.

Melt a small amount of butter in a non-stick pan over a low–medium heat. Once it is bubbling, dollop in the batter in batches and fry each side until golden brown.

Drain onto paper towels and finish with a sprinkle of salt flakes.

Serve each fritter with a couple of slices of smoked salmon, a light covering of the Marie Rose sauce and a squeeze of lemon, and garnish as desired.

above: *Zucchini Fritters with Smoked Salmon and Marie Rose*

SAUERKRAUT

preparation: *30–40 minutes* | fermentation: *4–8 weeks*

1 whole cabbage

2–3 tbsp table salt (see note)

IF YOU WANT TO MAKE lots of sauerkraut, pile up the cabbages and scale up the recipe: it's just cabbage and salt. Just one cabbage will, however, still make plenty, although the volume will reduce considerably when the salt takes out the water. 'Sauerkraut' is German for 'sour cabbage', yet it is thought to have originated in China. It's both delicious and a major source of beneficial gut bacteria, of which lactic acid bacteria is most dominant.

Proper fermenting vessels — either jars with airlocks or fermentation crocks — should be used for storing the sauerkraut. Both work to support the fermentation conditions: they don't let oxygen in but they let carbon dioxide out, and they also keep out contaminants.

On the other hand, if oxygen is allowed into the jars, it will destroy the anaerobic bacteria on which the fermentation process depends.

How much salt?

The amount of salt needed is 3% of the shredded cabbage weight. So, if your shredded cabbage weighs 1 kg (1000g), you will need 30g of salt.

If the shredded cabbages weighs 2 lbs (32 oz), you will need just under 1 oz (0.96 oz) of salt. A reliable set of scales is essential, as the ratio of cabbage to salt, by weight, is critical for the fermentation process.

Carbon dioxide is a by-product of that process and it must be released. If it is left to build up in the jars, it could cause them to explode.

So, invest in the proper equipment before fermenting cabbage or other vegetables.

METHOD: Choose a cabbage fully enclosed by its outer leaves, which once removed will reveal the softer leaves within. Don't wash the insides though; they should have been protected by the outer leaves and therefore clean, and the plant's own bacteria is beneficial for fermentation.

Once the outer leaves are removed, you can quickly rinse down the whole cabbage, then leave it at that.

Cut the cabbage into wedges and feed through a food processor, to cut them into 5 mm / ¼ in. slices. This can also be done with a knife, but the slices will have a more rustic appearance. Either way, the slices can then be gently pulled apart (shredded).

Next, place the shredded cabbage in a very large, clean tub and mix through the salt.

The process now is to really crush and work the cabbage with your hands; gloves are needed, as you will be getting your hands all in and around the cabbage and really

above: *working a large batch of cabbage, to make sauerkraut*

Sterilizing jars & implements

It's important to use sterilized jars and utensils. This can be done at a very high temperature in a dishwasher but that assumes they'll be used straight after the washing has finished. Another way is to first wash the lids, jars, and utensils with warm soapy water, rinse, then place in a cooking pot. Completely cover with warm water and then bring to the boil. Don't be tempted to put the jars into boiling water, as it will shock the glass. Boil for 15 minutes, then remove from the heat and allow everything to sit in the hot water until ready to use (for up to an hour — the jars should still be hot when filled with the sauerkraut). Use tongs to remove the items, taking care not to touch the inside of the jars or the lids or any part of the implements that will come in contact with the sauerkraut. One of the advantages of this method is the boiling water won't damage the rubber seals which are found on many preserving jars. The salt in the sauerkraut will also kill bad bacteria, but sterilization of the jars and lids is essential.

working the salt so the juices start to come out and the cabbage begins to soften: don't be timid! The process will take a good 5 minutes or more. You will know when it is ready when it seems there is no more water to come out.

Now it is time to stuff the cabbage into a sterilized fermentation vessel (see note at left).

To do this, use a sterilized spoon (or tongs or gloves) to transfer the sauerkraut to the vessel and then press it down very firmly after each spoonful, so the juice comes to the surface. Keep going until the vessels are almost full (leave only about 1cm / ½ in. unfilled at the top, so there is little room for air). Make sure the cabbage is fully covered by liquid (use sterilised culinary weights if you want), then seal.

Store the jars at room temperature (18°–25°C / 65°–77°F) and resist the urge to open them to check on progress: that will introduce oxygen and cause the sauerkraut to go mouldy. Just leave them be and have faith in the process.

After about a month, you can open the jars to check the progress, taking care to be quick and not to contaminate the contents (use a sterilised utensil or glove): have a smell, have a taste, have a look. It should have a pleasant smell, but a stale smell or signs of mould will obviously indicate a problem. Only check once or twice: don't open the jars too often!

Once the seal has been broken, the sauerkraut will keep for up to 6 months in the fridge. If you are, however, wanting a funkier, deeper, richer ferment, you can quickly re-seal the jars (no harm will be done at this point) and allow the sauerkraut to ferment for a few more weeks, but after too long a period the flavour will become very intense and possibly sour. In my opinion, the golden moment is at about 1½ months–2 months in: a little shorter in summer and longer in winter.

facing page: *Pickled Fennel (see p. 68)*

PICKLED FENNEL

cooking : *about 15 minutes*

4 whole fennels

4 cups white vinegar

2 cups water

2 ½ cups white sugar

2 tbsp fennel seeds

FENNEL HAS A LOVELY PIQUANT FLAVOUR with sweet hints of licorice and anise. Pickled fennel remains pleasantly crunchy and its zingy freshness pairs well with warm grilled meats or cool cured chacuterie.

METHOD: Trim off the green stalks and just the outer leaves of each fennel, to be left with a tidy bulb that you can hold with your hand.

Shave this on a mandolin, starting on one side and turning as you go, or slice finely with a sharp knife, so by the end you're left with only the core.

Place the vinegar, water, sugar and fennel seeds in a large pot and bring just to the boil, so that the sugar dissolves.

Fill sterilized jars with the sliced fennel (see sterilizing notes on p.66). Top up each jar with the hot vinegar liquid, being careful not to shock the glass (see note on p.175). Seal hot, then allow the fennel to cool completely in the fridge.

Once cooled, this pickle will last a couple months left sealed out of the fridge, but it will need to be refrigerated once opened. It should then be used within a week.

BABAGANOUSH

preparation : *30 minutes*

6 eggplants

8 garlic cloves, peeled

300g / 10oz tahini

2 tbsp olive oil, approx.

zest and juice of 2 lemons

a handful of fresh parsley

salt flakes & freshly ground pepper, to season

I LOVE BABAGANOUSH: velvety, smoky, eggplant blended with rich, flavoursome olive oil and imbued with garlic and seasonings. Many years spent living in the Middle East meant I was exposed to the very best of this delicious spread and watched it being made on many occasions: the process is simple enough, but the secret to success lies in the subtle details.

First is the quality of the ingredients: select your eggplants with care (see notes on p.51), choose best-quality olive oil, and use the freshest parsley you can find (freshly picked if possible). Be sure to slice, rather than chop, the parsley.

Also pay close attention to the charring process, allowing enough time for both the cooking and steaming stages. Add the parsley, lemon, and olive oil shortly before serving, not before, so their flavours stay fresh.

Babaganoush can be served as an accompaniment to grilled meat and vegetables, rolled inside wraps with salad, or mixed with hummus to make a dip, to mention just a few of many options. When serving it as a dip, I usually pair it with freshly-made sweet potato and beetroot crisps; their slight sweetness and crunchy texture complements the smooth, smoky babaganoush very well, and their vibrant, contrasting colours add a nice energy to the dish.

Another simple but favourite way to serve it is with freshly baked, hot garlic focaccia, which is much the same as the Turkish bread that is traditionally served with Middle Eastern dips.

METHOD: Carefully place the eggplant over an open flame. A barbecue or firepit is ideal, but alternatively this can be done on a stovetop over a gas flame.

Turn occasionally until the skins are fully burnt and the flesh feels soft throughout. This will take about 20 minutes, give or take. You can check by squeezing the eggplant gently: if it is ready, it should compress easily, like a firm sponge, and the skin is likely to split and some hot juices spurt out. Be careful not to burn yourself: gloves are recommended.

Once they are ready, place the charred eggplants in a bowl and cover tightly with cling wrap and then allow them to steam for about 10 minutes.

Meanwhile, prepare the other ingredients: crush the garlic; finely slice the parsley leaves; and juice and zest the lemons.

By this time, the eggplants should have cooled enough to handle. Peel and discard the skin and place the flesh into a pot. Cook down over a medium heat for about 5 minutes, to reduce the moisture content. Stir occasionally to make sure the flesh doesn't burn (reduce the heat slightly if necessary).

Transfer the eggplant to a bowl and allow it to cool. It should be very soft by now, so puréeing with a blender won't be necessary, but it is worth stirring around with the prongs of a fork to break up any lumps or stringy pieces — although a bit of texture is nice in this dish. Then use the fork to stir though the tahini, lemon juice, and a good glug of olive oil. Just before serving, add the zest and parsley, and season to taste.

Babaganoush is best served on the day it is made but otherwise will keep, covered, in the fridge for a day or two.

Beetroot & Sweet Potato Crisps

A little bit of vegetable goes a long way here, so you'll only need a couple of beets and maybe half a sweet potato to make a big plate of crisps. First prepare the sweet potato: give it a good wash then use a mandolin to evenly slice as much as you want (no need to peel), as thinly as possible. Place in cold water for an hour to remove excess starch, which will lead to a crispier result. Meanwhile, trim the roots off the beets and peel off any messy bits of skin and discard, and then rinse the bulbs and finely slice these as well. Next, heat 2½ cm / 1 in. of vegetable or canola oil in a deep pot to 170°C / 340°F. Drain the sweet potato on paper towels then begin frying all the vegetable slices in batches — in single layers so each one has plenty of oil in which to swim around. Fry until the bubbles stop (which means no water is left — this will take 3-5 minutes) and then, using a slotted spoon, lift them from the oil and drain in a single layer on paper towels. Sprinkle over with fine salt before the oil dries off so that it sticks, allow them to crisp up as they cool, then serve. Parsnip also works well cooked in this way.

facing page: *Babaganoush served with beetroot and sweet potato chips with a garnish of herbs*
following pages: *Blue Mountains National Park, New South Wales*

Chicken | Seafood | Duck | Trout

LEMON MISO CHICKEN *with* KIMCHI

cooking : *20–30 minutes*

1 tsp salt

2 large chicken breasts or 3–4 legs, skin on

1 tsp canola or grapeseed oil

1 tbsp white or yellow miso paste

1 tbsp honey

1 tsp vegetable oil

bunch of broccolini

2–3 tbsp lemon juice

dash of olive oil

1 cup kimchi, or to taste

THIS DISH IS BUILT ON contrasting flavours and textures: juicy chicken is matched to the acidity of the kimchi and the sweetness of the miso, while fresh broccolini provides an added crunch.

Miso and kimchi are fermented foods of Asian origin. Miso is made from soybeans, along with other ingredients such as rice, barley, and other grains. White miso is light and slightly sweet; yellow miso is earthy; and the deep red and even black misos have more intense umami flavours. White miso works well here because its soft sweetness complements the sour sharpness and crunchiness of the kimchi. Yellow miso can also be used, but the flavour of the darker misos will be too intense.

Kimchi is made from vegetables, usually cabbage but also others including carrots and radishes, along with garlic, chilli, ginger, and seasonings. In Korea, it is served at almost every meal: as a side dish or small meal, or added to other dishes such as soups and stews to boost flavour.

Long before fermentation was used to add flavour to certain foods it was a means to preserve them. Many people make their own and then store it in the fridge where it will keep for months, or even years. For this recipe, though, jarred kimchi, available at Asian grocery stores and many supermarkets, will work just fine.

METHOD: Set the oven to 200°C / 390°F, then rub the salt into the skin of the chicken.

Heat the oil in a large frypan over medium-high heat. It is important to use an oil with a high smoke point so it will not burn, and which also has a neutral flavour (canola and grapeseed oils work well).

Add the chicken, skin side down. After just a few moments, reduce the heat to low-medium and gently cook the chicken, without turning it, until the skin is nicely browned. Then turn the chicken over and sear on the other side for a few seconds, and then remove from the heat. The chicken should still be under-cooked, but well coloured.

Put the honey in a small saucepan and warm it over a low heat, so that it becomes runny. Mix in the miso and oil.

Brush the chicken on both sides and then place on a baking tray, skin-side up, and bake in the oven for 5 minutes or so, depending on the size, to complete the cooking process. The best way to check it is ready is to insert a thermometer into the thickest part of the meat. Once the temperature reaches to 73°C / 163° the chicken can be taken out of the oven. Place on a tray, so you can collect the juices as they rest for about 5 minutes.

In the meantime, blanch the broccolini for 2 minutes in salted, boiling water. Drain, and then toss them in a bowl together with the lemon juice and olive oil.

Thinly slice the rested breast against the grain, or leave the legs whole (if using). Pour over the reserved juices and serve alongside the broccolini and kimchi (about 1 good tablespoon per serve).

above: *Lemon Miso Chicken made with chicken legs and served with kimchi*

right:
Lemon Miso Chicken made with chicken breasts, served with kimchi (at the back of the plate), broccolini, carrots, and herbed garlic yoghurt

CHICKEN SHAWARMA

marinating : 2—24 hours | preparation and cooking : *a little over an hour, approx.*

for the chicken:

1 tbsp each cumin, cardamon & coriander, seeds or ground

1 tsp cayenne pepper

1 tsp cloves, seeds or ground

1 tbs vegetable oil approx.

8 chicken thigh fillets, skin off

additional oil, for frying

for the wraps:

½ iceburg lettuce

3–4 ripe tomatoes

1 white onion, peeled

½ tbsp pickles of your choice

continental parsley or coriander (cilantro)

1–2 drops of chilli oil, optional

flatbreads (see p. 80)

for the garlic yoghurt:

500 g / 1 lb Greek-style yoghurt

4–5 garlic cloves, peeled

1 tsp sumac

1 lemon

WHILE IN 5TH AND 6TH GRADES at primary school in Doha, Qatar, I would order a Chicken Shawarma and a Lipton lemon iced tea from the 'in-school food truck' every day, It was amazing every time and cost me only 7 riyale, which was about one Australian dollar.

This recipe is for nostalgia's sake; it is still a flavour that transports me back to my childhood.

METHOD: If the spices are already ground, just mix them together with a little bit of oil to form a paste.

Otherwise, toast the seeds of all the spices except the cayenne pepper in a dry pan until fragrant, stirring as needed, and then blitz into a fine powder in a blender. Pass this through a sieve to make sure you have a very fine spice mix, then mix it together with a little bit of oil, as above.

Preparing the seeds in this way will take longer but will give a deeper flavour, so it is worth the effort if you have time.

Place the chicken thighs in a dish and coat thoroughly with the spice mix. Cover and leave in the fridge to marinate for a few hours or, ideally, overnight.

This is a good time to make the garlic yoghurt ahead of time so that it is ready to serve later. Just crush or mince the garlic and stir it through the yoghurt together with the sumac. Juice the lemon and mix that through too, and you can also add some fresh lemon zest, as much or as little as you like.

Cover and refrigerate until ready to use.

facing page: *Chicken Shawarma, vegetables, flatbread and yoghurt, ready for wrapping*

Flatbreads

A wide range of ready-made ones are available at any supermarket and can be warmed quickly in a pan or microwave, but they are also quick and easy to make. One way is to mix 2 cups plain / all-purpose flour, a teaspoon of baking powder and some salt into 1 cup of greek yoghurt. Lightly knead on a floured bench, cover with kitchen film, and rest for 10–20 minutes. When ready to cook, cut into 4 portions and roll each one out into a thin disc. Cook one at a time in a pan over medium heat (oiled or not, depending on preference; oil will give a crispy rather than soft finish), until it begins to puff up. This will be quick! Now flip it over to the other side, brushing with oil if desired, until golden. Alternatively, cook them on a grill plate (you can do several at a time) over an open flame for added smoky flavours and a crisp and slightly charred surface: brush some olive oil on the grill plate then cook as above. Brush the tops with a little more oil while the undersides are cooking, before you flip them over to finish.

When you're almost ready to cook the chicken, first slice the onion finely and soak it in iced water for a couple of minutes to soften the sharpness. Then slice up the tomato and pickles and shred the lettuce. Arrange on a serving plate.

Now fry the thighs over a medium-high heat (either in a frypan on a stovetop or on a grill plate over an open flame), turning as needed, until just cooked. Chicken fillets must be cooked to 74°C / 165°F before consumption but you can take them off the heat at 73°C / 163°F because the temperature will rise a couple of degrees more while the chicken rests.

Cooking the chicken won't take long — 4–5 minutes on either side, depending on their size.

While the chicken is cooking, start cooking the flatbreads (if making your own), and cover in a clean towel to keep them warm as you cook the rest.

If using store-bought ones, warm them in a pan for a few seconds on both sides, or in the microwave.

to bring it all together : To assemble the wraps, take one flatbread at a time and layer down some lettuce, tomato, and pickles in the centre (not too much as it will make it too hard to wrap up).

Add a few pieces of chicken and top with a dollop of garlic yoghurt. They will shine even more with a dash of chilli oil if you have some to hand. Garnish with some freshly chopped parsley and / or coriander (cilantro) leaves.

The vegetables should be spread out towards the sides of the wrap, but not all the way — leave some extra bread at the edges to tuck in around the ingredients as you roll, to stop the wrap from leaking. One side can be left open to expose some filling if you like — provided the wrap is held upright. Roll up the wraps and enjoy.

facing page : *Chicken Shawarma, cooking in the pan*

JUICY FRIED CHICKEN

brining: *3-24 hours* | preparation and cooking: *about 30 minutes*

6 chicken thighs, skin on

for the brine:

500 ml / 2 cups water

15 g / ½ oz salt

15 g / ½ oz sugar

aromatics (e.g., bay leaves, peppercorns, coriander seeds), garlic cloves, to taste

for the batter:

4 eggs

200 g / 7 oz plain flour

100 g / 3½ oz corn flour

1 tbsp baking powder

1 tbsp paprika

1 tbsp turmeric

1 tbsp cumin

1 tsp onion or garlic powder

1 tsp salt

1-2 cups of oil, approx.

to serve:

burger buns, tomatoes, lettuce, chipotle mayonnaise, herbed yoghurt, etc.

BATTERED FRIED CHICKEN is very popular in the southern United States, including Texas where I lived for a large part of my teenage years.

The trick to its juicy magic is the use of a wet brine, and the trick to the brine is having the correct ratios: 100 parts water to 3 parts each — or 3% — of salt and sugar. Then it's a matter of adding the aromatics: maybe a couple of bay leaves, a tablespoon or so each of peppercorns and coriander seeds, and a couple of garlic cloves if desired. I also like to add juniper berries if I have them to hand, but 2 or 3 cloves also work well.

Brining is an easy but often over-looked step, perhaps because it takes some time or, misleadingly, sounds a bit 'salty', yet it will transform a basic dish into succulent, moreish cuisine. It does three things: it helps the meat retain moisture; it lightly cures the meat which improves texture; and it seasons the surface. I like to brine chicken for 24 hours, but even a few hours is worthwhile.

When it comes to the frying, choose a neutral, flavourless, oil that also has a high smoke point, so it will heat to a higher temperature without burning. Good options include canola and grapeseed oils.

METHOD: Bring the water, salt, sugar, and aromatics, to the boil, then turn off the heat and allow the flavours to infuse as the brine cools. Once the brine has cooled, place the chicken in a suitable resealable bag or container and fully cover with the brine. If you have lots of chicken, just divide it up into a couple of bags or containers as needed. Refrigerate for a few hours, ideally overnight and up to 24 hours.

When you are almost ready to cook, lift the chicken from the brine and pat dry with a paper towel.

Whisk the eggs in a large bowl and thin out with 2 or 3 tablespoons of water.

Separately, mix together the dry batter ingredients (flours, baking powder, spices, and salt). One at a time, dab each chicken thigh in the flour to coat it, shake off any excess, then dredge the thigh through the egg.

Now hold the thigh high above the egg mix for a few moments so any excess egg runs off, and then dab it in the flour once more.

Select a deep pot (or deep fryer) and add enough oil to submerge the chicken. This will depend on how much chicken you can fry at a time and on the size of the pot (you may need to fry in batches).

Working out brine ratios...

Where water is concerned, liquid measures convert easily to weights: 100 ml of water weighs about 100 g, and 30 fl. oz is equal to about 30 oz. This makes it simple to work out the percentage, by weight, of sugar and salt to put in your brine. It's not true of all liquids: many, such as oils, are heavier than water. Cold water is also slightly heavier than hot, so there is always some variance involved. Unless otherwise stated, these recipes assume the water is at room temperature.

This brine also works well for grilled or roasted chicken. If you have a lot of chicken, you'll need more brine. So, first work out how much water you need to cover the chicken completely, and from there work out how much salt and sugar is needed.

above: *bagging and sealing the chicken in brine*

To quickly cool the brine

To speed things up, think ahead and reduce the amount of water used in the brine, then add the missing weight of water in ice blocks just before popping it in the fridge. If adding, say, 225 g or about 8 oz of ice, you'll need to reduce the initial amount of water by a corresponding 225 ml or 8 fl. oz.

Chipotle Mayonnaise

Chipotle Mayonnaise is a made by mixing adobo and chipotles through mayonnaise. 'Adobo' is a hot, spicy tomato-based sauce of Mexican origin, and chipotles are dried and smoked jalapeño peppers. It's easy enough to make your own, but chipotles already mixed in adobo sauce can usually be found in the Mexican food section of most supermarkets. Just stir them through the mayonnaise, at a ratio of about 4 parts mayonnaise to 1 part of the chipotles -and-adobo mix, then adjust to taste.

The pot should only be about a third filled with oil, as there must be plenty of room for the oil to rise up and boil without bubbling over.

Heat the oil to 170°C / 340°F. To check, place the end of a wooden spoon in the oil. If bubbles form and rise up, the temperature is about right; if the bubbles are vigorous, it's too hot.

Next, use a deep-fryer basket to lower the thighs into the oil, or slide them in with a slotted spoon.

Fry for 10–12 minutes, until they are golden and cooked through, then carefully lift them out and drain on paper towels.

Serve in burger buns, with mayonnaise, tomato, and lettuce, or dipped in a herbed yoghurt sauce or served with chipotle mayonnaise: however you like to eat them.

above: *Juicy Fried Chicken served with chipotle mayonnaise*

CHICKEN *and* PUMPKIN RISOTTO

preparation and cooking : *1 hour 15 minutes*

1-2 tbsp olive oil

450g / 1lb pumpkin, peeled

1-2 tbsp butter

1 large onion, peeled & finely diced

3-4 garlic cloves, peeled & crushed

1 chicken breast, skin off

1 chicken thigh, skin off

6-8 button or portobello mushrooms, cleaned

4 cups chicken stock

good handful of baby spinach

2½ cups arborio rice

¼ cup white wine

1 cup freshly grated parmesan

1-2 tbsp toasted pine nuts

THIS IS MY MOTHER'S RECIPE, the first I learnt to cook and later copied from her notebook into my own. It is a real comfort meal, deeply satisfying, warming, and delicious, and one of the nicest things is how the sweet, buttery pumpkin 'mooshes' in with the creamy aborio rice, to make a rich, brothy mix.

It's important to use aborio rice (or carnaroli, if you want), because of how it contributes to the melded textures of a good risotto. Unlike other rices, it doesn't need to be washed, and it's better not to as that can affect its starches, which are key to its magic. Aborio rice needs to be toasted before adding any liquid, though. This helps it hold its shape and plays a part in the way in which the starches are released into the other ingredients.

There are many types of pumpkins from which to choose, but I favour Kents because they are readily available and hold their texture well when roasted (if not over-cooked). Smaller ones tend to be sweeter and easier to cut, which is better than wrestling with the thick skin of a larger pumpkin. Those with deep, orange flesh rather than pale also have the best flavour and texture, although that is hard to gauge unless the pumpkin has already been cut (but I don't like buying pre-cut pieces because some freshness is always lost).

So, choosing smaller pumpkins with deep-coloured skins is my rule of thumb. Butternut pumpkin also works quite well, but it never seems to give me the same depth of sweet flavour and caramelization in this dish as that provided by the Kents.

Toasting pine nuts

Oven-toasting gives a more even result than pan-toasting. Simply line a tray with baking paper and spread over with a layer of nuts. Bake in the 180°C / 350°F oven for 5–7 minutes. Watch them as they will burn easily, and if pressed for time a quick fry in a dry pan over a gentle heat — and with constant stirring — will work almost as well.

For this recipe, it is a good idea to dice the onion and crush the garlic a little ahead of time because your hands will be too busy stirring during the cook.

METHOD: Pre-heat the oven to 180°C / 350°F.

Pour the olive oil into a large pot. Dice the pumpkin into roughly 2½ cm / 1 in. chunks, and then toss them through the oil. You can use this same pot later to cook with, to reduce the amount of washing-up.

Spread the pumpkin out in one loose layer over the base of a shallow baking pan. Roast for 30–40 minutes, until the pumpkin has deepened in colour and begun to caramelize around the edges. It should be soft but not mushy. How much time it will take will vary depending on the pumpkin, so keep an eye on it (note too that it is likely to shrink noticeably in size as it cooks and loses moisture). Once it is ready, remove from the oven and put to one side.

Place a knob of butter (about a ½ tablespoon) in the pot and melt gently. Add the diced onion and sauté it in the butter until it begins to soften, then add the crushed garlic to the pot. You might need to reduce the heat slightly, as the garlic can easily burn. Sauté for a little longer, stirring as needed, until the onion is soft and almost translucent, then lift out the garlic and onion and put to one side.

Dice the chicken into generous chunks (4 cm / 1½ in.). Add another knob of butter to the pot and increase the heat to medium–high. Once the butter begins to foam, add the chicken and brown on all sides, then drop the heat back to low–medium and allow the chicken to cook, stirring as needed. This should only take a 2–3 minutes.

Avoid over-cooking as the chicken will toughen. To check it is ready, cut open a larger piece; it should be juicy but white, and with none of the gelatinous texture of raw chicken. Once the chicken is cooked, remove it from the pot and put to one side.

Remove excess stems from the mushrooms and discard. Cut the larger mushrooms into halves, keeping the small ones whole. Increase the heat under the pot to high, and add the mushrooms. Cook for 4–5 minutes, stirring as needed as they start to brown. They might release a lot of water, but if the pot is hot enough this should evaporate as the mushrooms cook. Otherwise, simply drain off any excess. Once nicely browned, remove them from the pot.

Now add the rice to the pot, toasting it gently over a low–medium heat before adding another knob of butter. When that butter has melted, return the onions and garlic to the pot and then deglaze with the white wine.

As the wine reduces, add the stock, ladle by ladle, stirring gently. Each ladleful should be half-absorbed before the next is added.

Continue adding the stock for 15–20 minutes until the rice is almost cooked: it should still have a gentle bite and most of the broth should have been absorbed, but the mixture should still be very moist.

Return the chicken to the pot together with the roasted pumpkin and mushrooms. There should be just enough brothy liquid left to help mix the chicken and pumpkin through the rice and bring together all the ingredients.

Add a little more stock if needed, along with the parmesan and pine nuts and mix through. If it begins to look a bit dry, add more butter and/or stock. The risotto should have a rich, creamy sauce, although if you like a 'brothier' base you can adjust the ratio of stock to butter at this step.

To finish, toss the spinach through until just wilted.

Season with salt and freshly ground pepper, and a splash or two of lemon juice to brighten the flavour.

Cleaning mushrooms

Care is needed when cleaning mushrooms because they soak up water. Commercially-grown ones come from sterile environments, so some gentle brushing may be all that is needed. Just to be sure, I like to plunge a few at a time into a bowl of cold water, then swirl them around for 10–15 seconds, before drying them quickly and gently with a paper towel (that will also remove any residual dirt), and then placing them stem-side up on a tea-towel so they can dry a bit more. Alternatively, they can be dried gently in a herb spinner. Only then to do I trim off the base of the stems, which might have absorbed some moisture in the washing process. Larger mushrooms need a bit more care than sturdy, compact button mushrooms or portobellos, as their gills are more exposed and they can also break easily.

above: *Confit Duck served with Orange, Fennel and Radicchio Salad*

TATHRA DUCK

curing : *12 hours or overnight* | preparation & cooking: *20 minutes or thereabouts*

2 duck breasts, skin on

a pinch of salt

ONE OF THE GREAT THINGS ABOUT this recipe is it is easy: there is no fiddling around with rendering the duck fat, the steps are simple, and a crispy-skinned and mouth-watering result is assured. It takes very little effort and just some time to allow the duck to rest in the fridge overnight.

This recipe gets its name from Tathra Place, a free-range farm in New South Wales dedicated to regenerative farming practices. They supply delicious and ethically farmed duck, along with many other meats, and are a supplier of choice for me. Of course, you can source your duck from your own favoured supplier — although free-range definitely gives a better flavour. I like to serve it with Orange, Radicchio and Fennel Salad (see p. 56), or with mushrooms and roasted garlic.

Tathra Duck variation

A lovely way to prepare duck is to use the confit method, which means to cook it very slowly and gently in fat. To confit duck legs, season the flesh then wrap the skin around the legs to resemble a 'lollypop'. Place in a deep tray and cover with rendered duck fat (use your own if you have to hand, otherwise store-bought will be fine). Cover the legs with a layer of baking paper and then a layer foil and bake slowly in the oven at 80°C / 176°F for about 8 hours. Once ready, remove the legs gently with a slotted spoon, strain the fat and save for future use. Raise the oven heat to 200°C / 390°F, return the legs to the oven and leave for 6 minutes or until the skin is crispy. Serve on a bed of Orange, Fennel and Radicchio Salad (p. 56).

METHOD: Pat the skin of the duck breast dry then turn the breasts over. Season with a good pinch of salt. Now use your hands to stretch out the skin on all sides, then place the breasts, skin-side up, in the fridge.

Leave uncovered and allow the breasts to season through for about 12 hours, or at least overnight. This is also a great way to dry out the duck skin, which will ensure it is crispy when cooked. Additionally, it means there is no need to render (melt) the duck fat before frying.

When you are ready to cook the duck breasts, place a heavy-based pan over low heat and drop in a good pinch of salt flakes. Lay the duck breasts skin-side down in the pan and allow them to warm up with the pan. Using a spatula (or other suitable utensil), press down on the breasts so that the skin stays properly in contact with the pan. Leave them to cook gently, skin-side down, until a good crisp skin and nicely coloured crust has developed. This should take 6–8 minutes, by which time the duck should be nearly but not fully cooked — about 90% of the way there. It should be at about 45°C / 112°F. Any excess melted duck fat that begins to collect in the pan during this time can be removed with a spoon or drained off into a dish on the side.

When the duck breasts are nearly cooked, flip them over to sear the other side. Insert a cooking thermometer into the thickest part of the meat. The temperature should be about 55°C / 131°F, and the breasts should look slightly more plump (this is due to the proteins in the meat tightening up and causing the meat to swell). You can complete the cook in a 200°C / 390°F oven for a few minutes, but watch them closely to avoid over-cooking.

Once cooked, allow the breasts to rest for a good 5–10 minutes during which time they will cook a little more. Duck should be cooked to a temperature of 75°C / 165°F. Using a sharp knife, slice the duck breasts on an elegant angle and serve.

above: *Tathra Duck served with mushrooms, roasted garlic, duxelle and spinach*

RIVER TROUT *with* BAKED POTATOES *and* ROMESCO SAUCE

preparation : *minimum 3 hours to heat oven* | cooking : *about 1 hour*

1 whole river trout

several all-rounder potatoes, 1–2 per serve

oil or duck fat, for roasting

1 spanish onion, peeled

½ fennel, stalks and outer leaves removed

1 lemon

small handful of basil leaves

Romesco Sauce (p. 187)

THIS IS A GREAT WAY to use a wood-fired oven for all the cooking stages of the meal: to burn the ingredients for the sauce, to bake the potatoes, and to bake the fish and infuse it with nice, smoky, natural flavours.

When baking vegetables in a wood-fired oven, it's always nice to use earthenware trays and pots. Earthenware comes in a lovely array of colours that complements the ingredients, and there's something wonderful, too, about mixing the elements of fire and earth to prepare delectable food. Once cooked, tantalising aromas fill the air and the earthenware will keep the food hot while emanating a gentle heat to the immediate surrounds. Not all earthenware can be used in a wood-fired oven, though, so check first that yours is suitable for cooking in the oven's high temperatures. Otherwise, cast-iron or tin cookware are also good choices, although some of the visual appeal might be lost.

METHOD : First get your wood-fired oven going, so that it has time to heat up to about 220°C / 420°F. This may take a few hours.

to make the Romesco Sauce: See the recipe on page 187. You can make this beforehand, or start making it when you first light the oven then finish it as the oven heats up.

to cook the potatoes : While the oven is heating up, cut the potatoes into medium-sized chunks. Place them in a large pot and cover with cold water. Add a good dash of salt and bring to the boil, then reduce to a vigorous simmer and cook for 5 minutes. Drain them off and toss well to rough

up the outsides of the potatoes. Spread them out on a baking tray. This allows them to steam-dry, for the best crusty results.

Meanwhile, get together some nice fat. Duck fat is great with potatoes, as everyone knows, but a vegetable oil will also work well if that is all that you have to hand. Use one that can withstand the heat and won't burn, such as canola or grapeseed. Put the fat, or oil, in a baking tray then place that in the oven and allow it time to warm up.

Once the fat (or oil) is nice and hot, take the tray from the oven and carefully toss through the potatoes. Return the tray to the oven and allow the potatoes to cook for about an hour, turning them once every 20 minutes or so. Note that to have the potatoes ready at the same time as your trout, you will need to put the trout in the oven about 20 minutes before the potatoes are ready.

Always cook the potatoes for a little longer than you think is needed. They will appear 'ready' when the outsides are crisp and golden and the insides soft and fluffy or even creamy, but continue cooking them for another 5 minutes beyond that point. Don't worry about the extra time: it's almost impossible to overcook potatoes provided they have enough fat to convert the starch into a delicious, crispy crust.

facing page: *River Trout with Romesco Sauce (potatoes not shown)*
above: *skewering the trout to check for doneness, Fuegos de Apalta, Chile*

Crispy potatoes tips

- *Choose good 'all-rounder' potatoes that sit between the waxy types on one hand and too-floury on the other. Pontiacs, désirée, and sebago are good options.*

- *Cook the potatoes twice, first by boiling (or steaming) to get the cooking of the insides underway, and second by roasting for a crispy crust. It is difficult to achieve both in one cook; you're more likely to end up with an under-cooked inside or an over-cooked crust, or even a potato that has become leathery.*

- *After the first cook, give them time to cool and dry. This creates a starchy outer layer that soaks up the fat during baking, to give a lovely crisp crust.*

- *Roughen up the edges of the cooled potatoes to create more surface area, which means more spots to soak up fat and so more crunch.*

- *Be generous with the oil or fat used for roasting: it increases the heat, leading to a quicker cook, and also works with that starchy outer layer to caramelize and crisp up the outsides. A ratio of 1 part fat or oil to 10 parts potatoes by weight is a good rule of thumb.*

to cook the trout: First wash the trout under cool water and rinse water through the insides. It should be left whole and on the bone, as this is a nice way of keeping the meat tender and rich when baking it in an oven.

Place most of the basil and some slices of lemon inside the fish so that the flavours infuse the fish nicely, but keep some back to use as a fresh garnish later. Then place the whole fish in an oiled baking tray (use olive oil), and then drizzle some more olive oil over the top. Season with salt flakes and freshly ground pepper to taste, then bake in the hot oven (220°C / 420°F as set for the potatoes), for about 15–20 minutes.

To judge if it is cooked, watch for the white proteins of the fish to set and seep out in little droplets. At the 15-minute mark, you can poke a thin metal skewer through the meat and check for any resistance, which you will feel as a kind of 'clicking'. (During my time working as a chef in Chile, I would cut a piece of wire every morning and wrap it around my finger, then use that to poke the fish. It was a very 'connected' way to test the fish, and gave me a greater ability to sense resistance — it's worth a try.)

Continue cooking as needed until there is no more clicking, by which time the flesh should be soft and the eyes white. Then take the fish from the oven and allow it to rest for 5 minutes, during which time it will continue to cook.

Lay the trout on a bed of very thinly-sliced onion and fennel, and a few split celery stalks, and stuff the cavity with the reserved slices of fresh lemon and thinly sliced basil leaves. Then the fish can be cut, and the flesh can be scraped off the bone with a spoon (leaving the skin behind). Serve together with the Romesco Sauce, which should be at room temperature, not chilled.

facing page: *Flametail Snapper with Cherry Tomatoes and Jerusalem Artichoke (recipe on p. 96)*

FLAMETAIL SNAPPER *with* CHERRY TOMATOES *and* JERUSALEM ARTICHOKES

preparation and cooking : *about 1 hour & 15 minutes*

2 snapper fillets, 200 g / 7oz each approx.

1 tbsp vegetable oil, for frying

for the vegetables :

150 g / 5 oz jerusalem artichoke

½ tsp curry powder, or to taste

6 cherry tomatoes

1 french shallot (eschalot)

2–3 tbs olive oil

½ tbsp balsamic vinegar, or to taste

2 tsp fresh lemon juice, approx.

salt & pepper, to season

for the tarragon salsa :

½ bunch of tarragon, or 1 small bunch

2–3 tbsp olive oil, approx.

1 tbsp lemon juice

to serve :

a few leaves frisée or radicchio

2 lemon wedges

THIS IS A LOVELY, LIGHT, simple dish, made with fresh snapper fillets that are then cooked quickly and easily. The recipe is also versatile — any nice white fish such as barramundi can be used, or river trout, if snapper isn't available. Either way, make sure the fish is as fresh as possible; fillet and portion yourself if you are comfortable doing that, or ask your fishmonger to do that at the time of purchase, not before.

This recipe is enough for at least two serves — it can be difficult to cook more than two fillets at a time unless you have a couple of pans on the go at once — but if you need more, simply increase the number of fillets and other ingredients in equal proportions.

You can also cook the fish on a medium-hot grillplate over an open flame, which makes it easier to do several at a time. Baking is another option, but it is harder to control the crispness of the skin so can be less successful.

Snapper has a mild, slightly sweet and quite nutty flavour that pairs nicely with the jerusalem artichoke, which also has a nutty flavour as well as some sweet notes. The name 'jerusalem artichoke' is confusing, though: it's not an artichoke (although related), and it is the root that is eaten, not the leaves.

Frisée is a lettuce-like vegetable with attractive leaves that catch sauces and dressings. It has a slightly bitter flavour that balances the sweetness of the other vegetables. Radicchio also works well as a substitute.

Balsamic vinegar is unbeatable for the sticky, sweet and mildly acidic finish it gives to the tomatoes.

METHOD: First set the oven to 200°C / 390°F and allow it time to warm up.

to prepare the vegetables : Start with artichokes and give them a good wash, as dirt can hide in the nooks can crannies. Tidy them up by slicing off any dark spots and large knots. Other than that, they shouldn't need peeling.

Cut them into smaller chunks (roughly 2 cm / ¾ in.). As you do that, make a point of cutting through those harder-to-reach areas, just so you can make sure no dirt has been missed. Toss the pieces in a bowl with a tablespoon or so of the olive oil, and a pinch each of curry powder and salt.

Lay them out on a baking tray, cover with foil, and bake them for about an hour, until they are soft all the way through.

above: *jerusalem artichoke*

Meanwhile, rinse the cherry tomatoes then toss them in some olive oil, enough to coat, together with the balsamic vinegar and a pinch each of salt and pepper. Once the artichokes are nearly done, at about the 50-minute mark, you can add the tomatoes to the oven. It's better to put them in a separate tray, otherwise if they burst their liquids will flow onto the artichokes. Bake the tomatoes until they just begin to burst, then remove them from the heat.

While the artichokes and tomatoes are roasting, cut the french shallot in half and lay it cut-side down in a dry pan over medium-high heat and cook until the cut side is completely burnt. This will take a couple of minutes or so.

Remove from the pan and allow to cool slightly, then pull it apart gently, but without breaking it. It should stay intact, to leave you with two small, charred cups.

To prepare the salad: Prepare the dressing, a tarragon salsa, ahead of time, so that it is ready when you come to serve the dish. Using just the tarragon leaves, slice them into thin, elegant strips and mix them with the olive oil and lemon juice. Don't make the mixture too oily: there should be enough tarragon to make it quite chunky, more the texture of a salsa verde rather than a vinaigrette.

To cook the snapper: You can start cooking the snapper a few minutes before taking the tomatoes and onions from the oven, so everything can be served hot.

Season the skin and flesh of the fillets with salt, then heat a little oil in the a pan over medium—high heat. Lay the fillets skin-side down in the pan. You'll need to press down on them to ensure there is good skin contact with the pan, otherwise the skin will not cook evenly and will curl up.

Cook the fish 70% of the way through on this side, by which time the skin will have deepened in colour and the flesh just above the skin begun to turn white. Small white spots of protein will start seeping from the fish. It will usually take 2–3 minutes to reach this point. Now turn it over and cook for a minute or a little more on the other side, then remove from the heat. Use the skewer test as described on page 94 to check if it is done. Alternatively, check the internal temperature. The Food Safety Information Council of Australia recommends that fish fillets should be cooked to a temperature of around 63°C / 145°F or to when the flesh flakes easily

To serve, lay down the frisée and cover with the roasted vegetables. Lay the cooked snapper alongside and garnish with a fresh lemon wedge. Serve the tarragon salsa on the side, or over the vegetables.

MISO SALMON

marinating : *10 minutes minimum, up to 24 hours* | preparation and cooking : *about 30 minutes*

for the marinade :

50 g / 1⅔ oz red miso

1 tbsp sake

1 tbsp mirin

20 g / ⅔ oz brown sugar

for the salmon :

1 salmon fillet per serve, skin off

steamed Asian greens (e.g., bok choy, kai lan, white cabbage, pea shoots)

sprinkling of sesame seeds, toasted or raw, to taste

ALTHOUGH THIS IS A LOVELY LIGHT MEAL, it has the punchy earthiness of red miso, which is balanced by the two rice wines: the sweet, almost syrupy mirin, and then the more astringent, cleansing sake.

METHOD : Put all the marinade ingredients into a pot. Bring to the boil and cook until the mixture has slightly thickened. This will take about 5–10 minutes.

Brush the salmon with the marinade and allow it to sit for at least 10–15 minutes, or up to 24 hours.

Pre-heat the oven or grill plate to 200°C / 390°F. Place the fillets on a baking tray or grill and bake for 8–10 minutes, depending on their size, until they reach an internal temperature of 60°C / 140 °F.

If you don't have a meat thermometer handy, you can test with a metal barbecue skewer: just insert it into the thickest part of the fillet, leave it there for a moment, then remove it and immediately place against your hand. If it feels hot, the fish is ready to be removed from the heat. If it is cool or mildly warm, more time is needed.

Aim to remove the fish just before it is fully cooked, and then allow it to rest for 5 minutes before serving, so it cooks a little longer. Cooked fish should be opaque with firm meat that flakes easily. Undercooked fish will be soft and translucent in places.

Serve the salmon with steamed Asian greens and a sprinkling of sesame seeds.

following pages : *grazing land on farms of the Central West highlands of New South Wales*

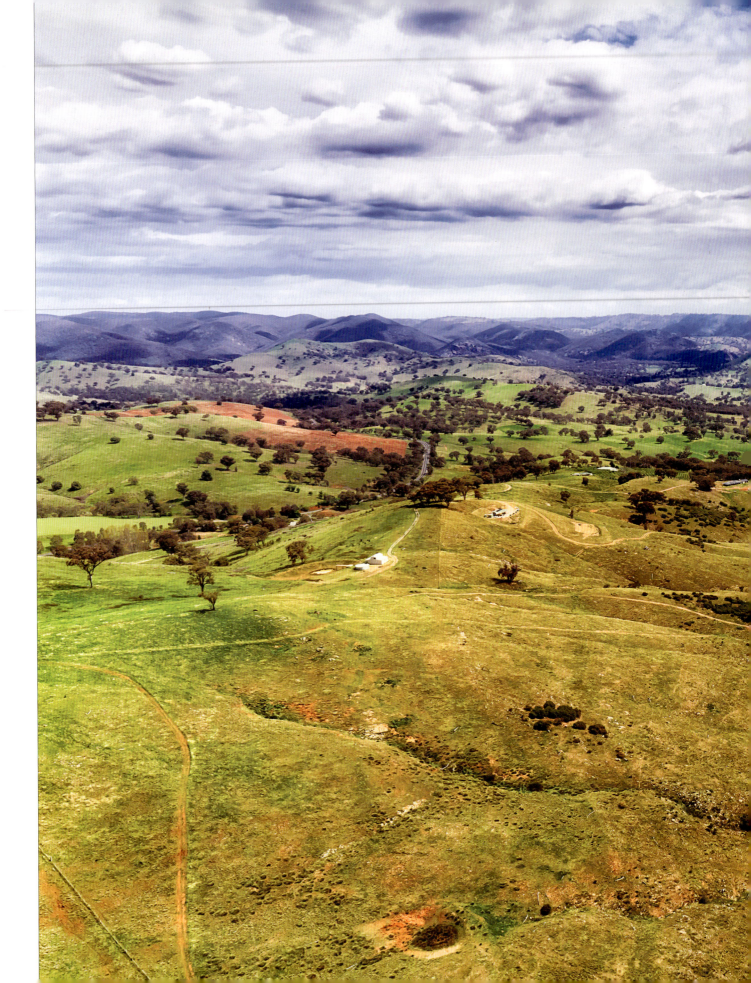

Beef | Pork | Lamb

STEAK TARTARE

preparation: *10–15 minutes*

*eye fillet, ultra-fresh,
1 (gloved) handful per serve*

½ eschalot per serve

1 small cornichon per serve

1–2 scapes per serve

egg yolks, 1 per serve, optional

worcestershire sauce

capers, to taste, optional

few sprigs of continental parsley

a few croutons, optional

Scallions, spring onions, eschalots, and shallots

There is some inter-changeability with these terms, depending on who you are speaking with. Broadly, 'spring onions' are those with long green stems and a small, white bulb, barely wider than the stem. They are known as scallions in the US. Eschalots are small, oval-shaped onions with thin, brown skins. They are sometimes called 'french shallots', noting that the word 'shallot' is also sometimes used in place of 'spring onion'.

STEAK TARTARE IS A FRENCH DISH made from very finely sliced raw beef, traditionally served with a fresh egg (yolk only) broken over the top. Very fresh, highest-quality, chilled tenderloin (eye fillet) will be needed — use the tail or the small pieces trimmed off when preparing the fillet for another dish.

Make sure any fat, sinew, and loose skin is removed.

There are a few rules: make sure all utensils and other equipment such as chopping boards are spotlessly clean; wear culinary gloves, as you will be handling meat and it won't be cooked; work quickly and make sure the beef stays chilled at all times; serve immediately, or at least within 30 minutes of making; never be tempted to use mince in place of fresh meat; and remember that Steak Tartare can't be stored. It is to be eaten when it is made.

To help ensure the quality and freshness of the meat, purchase from a reliable butcher and let them know that you intend to use it for Steak Tartare.

When it comes to flavour, I like to add in 'scapes', which are the stems of the onion or garlic flowers. They have a lovely flavour, a bit more intense than eschalot. The thicker, middle part of the stem has the best flavour, while closer to the flower it can become too sharp or intense. If you can't find any scapes, you can substitute onion or garlic chives, or both.

METHOD: Leave the meat in the fridge so it stays cool as you gather and prepare all your other ingredients.

Finely chop ('brunoise') the eschalot and cornichons into tiny dice, and then finely slice the scapes. Mix all together in a bowl.

Take the fillet from the fridge and, using a sharp knife, slice the steak very finely against the grain, and then cut the slices into thin strips (no more than 3 mm / ⅛ in.). Now cut the strips into a fine dice. Add the beef to the bowl with the diced vegetables and stir through the tartare sauce. At this point, the dish should be plated; a small handful makes a usual serve and this can be arranged on the plate in a nice mound (moulds aren't necessary). If adding egg yolk, you can make a small hollow in the top and break it in (just the yolk).

Top with some parsley (finely chopped) and add a splash of worcestershire sauce, a few capers (if using), and some croutons, which will add a nice, contrasting crunch.

Croutons

Thinly slice some day-old bread — baguettes work well and the slices will be the right size (not too big). Cover the base of a large baking tray with a thin film of olive oil then lay out the slices in a single layer on top. Drizzle some more olive oil over them, then bake in a 180°C / 350°F oven for 8 minutes. Remove from the oven and sprinkle over with sea salt and allow the croutons to crisp up as they cool. The idea is they form little scoops from which to eat your tartare.

above: *Steak Tartare, served with fresh croutons made from a baguette*

RAGÙ ALLA BOLOGNESE

preparation & cooking : *minimum 3 hours*

1-2 tbsp chicken, beef, or duck fat

2 large brown onions, peeled

2 carrots

3 celery stems

1 bay leaf

a few sprigs of thyme

1-2 tbsp olive oil

1 kg / 2 lb pork & beef mince, 50/50 split

100 / 3 oz chicken livers, optional

4 tbsp tomato paste

1 head of garlic

⅔ cup red wine, approx.

2 tins of tomatoes, each 400g / 14 oz or thereabouts

2 tbsp sugar

1 red chilli, optional

8 cups beef or chicken stock

extra butter, for warming

salt & pepper, to season

lemon juice, freshly chopped parsley, & freshly grated parmesan, to serve

RAGÙ ALLA BOLOGNESE, or 'Bolognese sauce', is from the food capital of Italy, Bologna, an historic city in the Emilia-Romagna region whose many nicknames include 'Bologna la grassa', or 'Bologna the fat', on account of its rich cuisine. A 'ragù', generally, is a meat sauce, and variations are found all over Italy. Traditionally, the ragù of Bologna includes less tomato — and sometimes none at all — than the Australian adaptations.

It can be served on the day it is made, but it unfailingly tastes better the following day, after the flavours have had the chance to develop and meld.

My paternal grandfather was fond of this sauce and, when making it for his delicate lasagne or even for a simple pasta meal, he liked to use rump steak which he would sear in one large piece on a hot skillet or barbecue plate before allowing it to rest for a short time. He would then slice it very finely against the grain, using a razor-sharp, specially whetted knife, before adding it to his gently simmering base.

His method was heavily influenced by those of his own parents, both from Tuscany, and he would often say the most flavoursome ragùs he ever tasted were made by Italian women, such as his mother Bruna, who would casually toss left-over chunks of meat from previous meals — often veal and pork as well as beef — into a heavy-based pot, usually with a generous slab of butter or other fat, and allow them to cook down slowly with the other ingredients over many hours, during which time the meat would break up to form a rich sauce.

facing page: *Piazza Maggiore, Bologna, Italy, 2023*

Chicken livers

Like many other cuts of meat, chicken livers have sinew (connective tissue) running through them which can be white, pink, or even slightly green in colour. This needs to be removed before cooking, but it is easily done.

First, unroll the livers (if they are folded over).

Next, place them in a large bowl of cool water, so they are quite spread out, for about 15 minutes. This isn't an essential step, but makes the following ones easier.

Drain off the bloodied water and lay the livers out flat on a chopping board. Blot with paper towels to dry and wipe off any bits of remaining blood.

Using a small, sharp knife or scissors, trim off and cut out the sinew and discard. There can be quite a bit running through the liver, so just take your time. As the liver is to be used in a sauce, you can of course cut the meat into small pieces as you go, making it easier to reach the sinew.

He chose not to use mince because he thought it gave a dry result, but that was probably because he used a low-fat beef mince. Fattier mince is better here, and a mixture of pork and beef works particularly well. The detail, though, that left-over cold cuts can be added to the sauce is worth noting.

Chicken livers are traditionally used in this ragù and will add a luscious richness, but it comes down to taste. Some chefs use a large amount (up to half the beef quantity, as in Elizabeth David's recipe), and others very little or none at all. If the mince is on the dry side, livers will certainly enhance the results.

If using more liver than suggested here, you should cut back on the pork mince so the pork and livers combined are about equal to the weight of the beef mince.

This sauce is typically used in pasta dishes (spaghetti, lasagne, cannelloni, etc.), but also with rice in a risotto, and in other ways, such as a stuffing for roasted capsicums. If serving with spaghetti, it's important to warm the required portion of sauce in the pot first, and then toss the pasta through it rather then dole the sauce over it as is the usual Australian way (although an extra spoonful over the top can always be added, to finish).

This recipe makes a generous amount, even though it will reduce significantly over the cooking time. Left-over sauce will keep in the refrigerator for up to 3 days, or frozen for up to 3 months.

METHOD: If you are going to use livers, first place them in cool water to soak (see note).

Meanwhile, in a large pot, gently melt the fat over a medium-low heat. Finely dice the onion, carrot, and celery and gently sauté in the fat until they begin to soften This is known as a 'soffritto' in Italy but it is much the same as the 'mirepoix' of French cuisine. It is a widely used base for numerous dishes.

Tie the bay leaves and thyme together with some string and add them to the pot.

Allow the vegetables to soften a little more, stirring as needed, but they should not become too coloured.

Once ready, use a slotted spoon to lift them from the pot and place to one side.

Increase the heat to medium–high and add a splash of oil to the pot (or some more fat if you have it to hand). Add the mince, using a wooden spoon to break it up, and stir it as it browns. It's important not to crowd the pot, so you can cook in two or three batches if necessary (topping up the oil or fat as needed). This will help ensure a nice caramelization occurs, whereas too much mince in the pot at once will take out heat and cause the meat to stew.

Once all the mince has been nicely browned and all of it returned to the pot, you can add a generous sprinkle of salt, to season. Don't do this while the meat is browning, as that will draw moisture out of the meat, which will also cause it to stew.

At this point, you should finish preparing the chicken livers, if using. Follow the notes on page 106 and, once all the sinew has been removed, finely dice the livers in readiness for cooking.

Remove the cooked mince from your pot and put to once side. Add the diced liver to pot, add a splash of oil if needed, and cook out for 2–3 minutes, stirring as needed. You may need to reduce the heat a little.

Next, return the mince to the pot. Crush or grate the garlic and add to the pot, together with the sautéed vegetables and tomato paste. Increase the heat to high, and cook for 1–2 minutes, stirring constantly.

Add the red wine, and use this to deglaze the base of the pot. Reduce the heat to a simmer and wait a few moments until the sharp scent of alcohol has subdued.

De-seed and finely dice the chilli (if using) and then add this to the sauce, together with the tinned tomatoes, sugar and stock. Bring the sauce back to the boil for a few moments, then turn it right down. Give it a good stir and allow it to simmer very gently on a low heat for several hours — at least 3 — until it has formed a rich, thick sauce, stirring now and again to clean all edges of the pot.

Alternatively, you can transfer the sauce to a slow cooker and leave on a medium setting for a few hours, checking on it as needed.

Once the sauce has reached the desired consistency, remove the bay leaf and thyme sprigs and allow the sauce to cool. Transfer to a suitable container, seal, and then store in the refrigerator, ideally overnight. The flavours will continue to meld.

If you are using the sauce to serve with spaghetti, first cook the pasta in salted water until 'al dente'. Reserve a tablespoon or two of the starchy pasta water before draining (more if you are making a large batch of spaghetti — you will need to use your own judgement here). Then, over a medium heat, melt a generous knob of butter in the pot and add the desired portion of sauce. Mix through the pasta water, a tablespoon at a time, and stir for a few minute or two; it will add a smooth, additional creaminess to the texture, but be careful not too add too much or the sauce may become too watery or even gluggy.

Add the lemon juice and chopped parsley for a fresh zing, then toss through the cooked pasta. Serve immediately, topped with grated parmesan (if using).

above: *food store in the Quadrilatero, Bologna's oldest market, 2023*
facing page: *Via dell'Indipendenza, Bologna, 2023*

BEEF TENDERLOIN *in* MISO MARINADE

marinating: *12–24 hours* | **preparation and cooking:** *20–30 minutes*
— if cooking over hot coals, allow plenty of time for coals to heat up

1 whole beef tenderloin

5 generous tbsp white miso paste

6 garlic cloves, peeled

50 g / 1½ oz ginger

1 small bunch of thyme

6 bay leaves

1 tbsp juniper berries

1 tbsp black peppercorns

2 cups vegetable oil

⅔ cup soy sauce

Carpaccio

This is an Italian dish made from, traditionally, wafer-thin slices of raw, fresh beef drizzled over with fresh lemon juice and olive oil. It is sometimes also prepared with raw fish and, less traditionally, with vegetables and fruit. It is normally served as an appetizer before a larger meal.

THIS IS A SIMPLE DISH best cooked on a hot grill plate or over a wood firepit or campfire, but it will also work nicely on a barbecue and even cooked indoors on a stovetop.

It takes some time to marinate, but the delicate, slightly charred flavours of tender, thinly sliced, warm fillet will be perfectly complemented by the tart notes of juniper and nips of garlic and ginger.

Unlike cooking a piece of steak, cooking an entire fillet is a relatively long, slow cook and can be expected to take up to half an hour, or even longer for large fillets.

I use dried junipers in this recipe, which don't need re-hydrating as they will be steeped in the marinade. Fresh or frozen ones can also be used, when available.

When cooking a whole tenderloin (also known as 'eye fillet'), it is important to make it as regular a thickness as possible, to ensure an even cook. These fillets always have a narrow tip, or tail, and are thickest through the centre. The tail, usually about a quarter of the length of the entire fillet, is sometimes tucked under, to help form the fillet into a more regular shape, but I prefer to trim it off. It is not the best part of the fillet and is often quite sinewy, but it can be used —immediately— for other dishes that use finely cut, fresh beef such as Steak Tartare or Carpaccio (see p. 102). It is likely those dishes evolved as a means to use the offcuts, and that is certainly the way of many restaurants where quality ingredients are never wasted.

Additionally, there are side muscles, referred to as the 'chain' meat, which should also be trimmed off. This is

facing page: *the final stages of cooking, when the tenderloin is elevated to reduce the heat*

really for no other reasons than they thicken the centre of the fillet too much and, conversely, because they can partially or fully detach from the main part of the fillet and then cook too quickly.

The chain meat can also be used for Steak Tartare or Carpaccio, and in dishes where smaller pieces of high-quality, finely sliced beef is needed. It was also a tradition in my father's family to incorporate the offcuts into beef ragùs (see p. 105).

The silver skin needs to be shaved off with a sharp knife, as should excess lumps of fat, all of which should be discarded (or fed to an appreciative pet). Thin strips of fat along the surface don't need to be removed and can assist with cooking, but larger pieces will become greasy. Sometimes it is worth cutting 2 or 3 shallow slashes across those thin outer layers of fat, otherwise the fat can buckle under the fillet as it cooks, causing it to take on an awkward shape that is also more difficult to slice.

METHOD: Rub the tenderloin all over with the miso paste. Separately, finely slice the garlic and ginger and place them in a mortar-and-pestle, together with the thyme (large stems removed), bay leaves, juniper berries, and peppercorns. Using a few drops of the vegetable oil, lightly crush the ingredients into a coarse mix. Rub this into the fillet, over the top of the miso paste.

Place the fillet in a large, strong, ziplock bag, and then add the soy sauce and remaining vegetable oil. Seal the bag and then use your fingers on the outside to lightly massage the marinade into the fillet for just a few moments, to ensure it is fully covered. Place in the refrigerator to marinate overnight.

When you are ready to cook the fillet, pre-heat the hot plate until it is hot, remembering that if you are cooking over coals you will need to allow plenty of time for them to heat up beforehand.

Remove the fillet from the ziplock bag (reserving the marinade) and place it on the grill plate. Slowly turn it along its length to sear it on all sides.

Allow it to cook, basting occasionally with the marinade to ensure the surface remains moist. Resist the temptation to turn the fillet again. If the underside is at risk of becoming charred you might need to reduce the heat a little. On a stovetop, this is easy: just lower the temperature to medium and continue to monitor the cooking: you can always increase the heat again if needed. If cooking over a woodfire, it can require a bit more intuition, which comes with careful monitoring of the meat and practice. You will need to either move the meat to a part of the hotplate which is not so hot, or adjust the coals below to allow the temperature to reduce. Most likely, it will be a combination.

At about the 10-minute mark, take a moment to insert a meat thermometer into the centre of the fillet. It should be nearing 30°C / 86°F but, if not, allow it to cook a little longer, before turning it over, just the once, and allowing it to continue cooking until the internal temperature reaches about 40°C / 104°F.

Then, to finish the cook, remove the fillet from the direct heat source. If cooking over an open flame, it should be elevated well above on a high grill plate and then rotated and basted frequently until cooked to the desired level (see notes on p. 24). If cooking on a stovetop, reduce the heat to medium and follow the same process. Wrapping the fillet in foil can also help at this stage, keeping in mind that we're not aiming for a crust on the fillet here.

Remove the fillet from the grill plate and wrap in foil (if you have not already done so). Allow it to rest, close to the fire so it stays warm but not hot, for about half an hour, then slice thinly to serve. As always, the meat will continue to cook and increase in temperature by a few degrees during this time.

above: *sliced to serve*

FIREPIT STEAK *with* CRIOLLA

preparation: *about 3 hours including heating the coals* | **cooking**: *about 10 minutes*

250–300 g / 8–10 oz sirloin steak

salt flakes & freshly cracked pepper, to season

1 tbsp vegetable oil, approx.

for the salsa:

2 green apples

1 red chilli

1 yellow, 1 red & 1 green capsicum

2 tomatoes

2 spring onions (scallions)

2 tomatoes

1 tbsp sherry vinegar

splash of fresh lemon juice, to taste

60 ml / 2 fl. oz olive oil

salt & pepper, to season

I LEARNT HOW TO MAKE this spicy, fruity, tangy salsa when working for Francis Mallmann in South America. During this time, I bought a very thin paring knife, but one of the chefs would always steal it away when he wanted to make this particular garnish. The role of sharp knives in kitchens can never be over-stated, and one is needed here to dice the ingredients very finely and cleanly, without crushing them.

The garnish itself is of South American origin. Along with its other flavours and textures, the chilli gives it a nice kick, but how much of one will largely depend on the type used. How much heat is needed in a dish, and the burning question of whether or not to remove the seeds (which adds to heat) comes down to personal taste. I generally remove them because too much heat can overwhelm other flavours, and their texture is not always compatible with other ingredients — but leave them in if you like.

I like to serve the criolla with sirloin, which has a flavour and texture better suited to the freshness of this sauce than fattier cuts of meat. This recipe uses, roughly, a ¼ kilogram / ½ pound of meat, or 1–2 steaks, depending on their size, which is enough for 3–4 serves. The salsa recipe will make about 1 cup, but you can always scale it up if you want more. It should be served soon after making though, so don't make more than you need.

This dish works best when the steak is cooked in the fresh air over a firepit or wood barbecue. That is part of the experience.

above: *the firepit and criolla*

METHOD: Light your firepit and allow it to burn down until the coals are grey–white and there is little flame. Do this well ahead of time as it takes a couple of hours to develop a hot coal base below your grill plate, which is needed to achieve a nice crust on your steak.

The grill plate also needs plenty of time to heat up: it must be hot.

to prepare the steak: About an hour before your cook, remove the steak from the fridge, pat it dry, and season evenly with salt.

Cover and allow it to come up to room temperature (about 25°C / 70°F). This can take an hour or more, depending on size.

to prepare the criolla: Meanwhile, core and de-seed the capsicum and apples, remove the skin, and de-seed the chilli. Dice into small, even-sized pieces and mix together.

Quarter the tomatoes and remove the seeds and watery flesh, to leave just the skin. Dice this together with the spring onion, to about the same size as the other ingredients, and add to the mix. Dress with the olive oil, vinegar, lemon juice, salt and pepper, adjusting to taste as needed.

to bring it together: First, make sure your grill plate is hot enough: it needs to be around 260°C / 500°F to properly sear the steak. If you can't check with a thermometer, you can carefully place your hand, with an open palm, about 8 cm / 3 in. above the grill plate (see p. 22 for more details). If you can only keep it there for 1–2 seconds before it becomes too uncomfortable, the grill is hot and you are ready to go. If you can barely keep your hand there for a full second, it is likely too hot.

Now dab the steak dry again (some more moisture would have come out from the earlier salting), then rub lightly with vegetable oil and season lightly again. Place it on the grill plate and leave it untouched for about 3 minutes to develop a good crust. Flip once and cook for a further 3–4 minutes or to your personal liking (see p. 25 for guidance).

Once you see some blood start to sit on the surface of the steak, it has reached a nice, medium–rare state, which I prefer. It is generally not recommended to cook steak beyond medium as it will become dry and it loses flavour, yet nevertheless some people like a well-done steak: each to their own.

You can also use a digital thermometer to track the internal temperature. Note that steak will continue to cook once removed from the heat, rising in temperature as it rests. You should therefore remove the steak from the heat when it is about 3–5 degrees below the ideal internal temperature, depending on thickness. The thicker the steak the more it will cook as it rests.

Serve dressed with the criolla.

Cooking steak: to flip or not?

Many claim that flipping just once gives an even cook and reduces the risk of juices escaping and the meat drying out, and enables a nice, caramelized crust to develop, while flipping disturbs the crust. Others say flipping several times reduces the cooking time and therefore the risk of the steak drying out, while still cooking it evenly (because it stops one side cooling as the other is cooked) and allowing for a crust to develop. It comes down to preference and can also depend on the thickness of the meat. If flipping just once, having the meat at room temperature first is important as it will reduce the cooking time and will also ensure the surface of the meat is not too moist. Generally, for a room-temperature steak that is 3–4 cm / 1–1½ in. thick, minimal flipping is needed. For larger or colder pieces of meat, an extra couple of flips or shifting the steak to a slightly cooler section of the grill plate after searing might reduce the risk of over-cooking.

For me, I like to limit interference so generally I avoid extra flipping as much as possible. My general rule of thumb is if the steak is sticking, it's not ready to flip!

facing page: *the seasoned steaks on the grill plate*

SCOTCH FILLET *with* PEPPER *and* MUSHROOM SAUCE

preparation: *1 hour* | cooking: *15–20 minutes*

for the steak:

2 scotch fillet steaks

1 tbsp olive oil, approx.

salt flakes

freshly ground pepper

for the sauce:

1 onion, peeled

3 cloves of garlic, peeled

100 g / 3½ oz portobello mushrooms

100 ml / 3 fl. oz white wine

60 ml / 2 fl. oz cream

lots of freshly ground pepper

salt flakes, to taste

parsley or tarragon, to garnish

THIS IS AN ABSOLUTE CLASSIC and a favourite of mine: a nice cut of scotch fillet, seared over an open flame with nothing but salt and pepper and a few splashes of olive oil, then dressed with a peppery mushroom sauce. I like to serve it with Pear, Walnut and Blue Cheese Salad (p. 28).

So the sauce is ready at the same time as the steaks, cut up the onions, garlic, and mushrooms as the meat is coming up to room temperature, then start making the sauce as the meat cooks. Add the cream just before serving.

METHOD: First, be sure to allow plenty of time to build up the hot coals and heat the grill plate.

Meanwhile, a good hour or so before cooking, remove the steaks from the fridge and pat dry with paper towels. Rub in the olive oil and then sprinkle generously with the salt and pepper on both sides. Use more than you think might be needed: it will be worth it. Then allow the steaks to sit as they come up to room temperature.

to cook the steak: When the grill plate is good and hot, dab the steaks again with paper towels and then place them on the plate. Allow them to cook on one side for 3–4 minutes, and then turn and cook on the other for a further 3–4 minutes, depending on whether you like your steak to be cooked rare, medium-rare, or medium (see p. 25).

The grill plate needs to be hot the entire time to ensure the steak sears properly and does not stew. If the steak is at risk of burning, you can reduce the heat a little after the initial searing, then increase it again before searing on the other side. Over an open flame, adjusting the heat will entail moving the steak to a slightly cooler, yet still hot, section of the plate or shuffling the coals underneath. Judging at what point the meat might be cooking too quickly or too slowly is quite intuitive but, really, if the temperature is not hot enough the meat will turn a grey colour rather than caramelize and it will lose water, which will then bubble around on the plate and stew the meat. If the meat is cooking too quickly, the crust will caramelize too much and even begin to thicken and char while the rest of the meat will be under-cooked.

Some chefs turn the steaks over a few times to prevent stewing on one hand and over-cooking on the other. I prefer to turn them just once and then shift their position or adjust the heat to control the process (see note on p. 117). Trial and error is very useful here.

Once the steaks are at the desired level of 'doneness', transfer them to a plate and cover them loosely with foil. Leave to rest in a warm spot for 4 minutes before serving.

to make the sauce : Finely dice the onion and then grate (or mince) the garlic. Clean the mushrooms and remove excess stems (see p.87) and then slice them finely.

Sauté just the onion in the olive oil over a low-medium heat until soft. Next, add the mushrooms and cook down slightly until they are nicely softened — about 2–3 minutes — and then deglaze with the white wine.

Give the sauce a few moments for the alcohol to cook off and for its scent to pass. Add the garlic and simmer gently for 5 minutes, allowing the aromas to open up. Just before serving, add the cream and herbs, bring quickly to the boil, then remove from the heat. Pour into serving jugs or directly over the rested steaks so serve.

Salt notes

Salt flakes are large salt grains, making it easier to sprinkle them quickly and evenly, while table salt can land in clumps or spread out too finely. It can also be hard to see, making it difficult to gauge whether a section of meat is over-salted or not salted at all. Salt flakes also dissolve more slowly, to give a more satisfactory and evenly-seasoned result. Kosher salt and Parrillera salt (used in South America) are other larger-grain alternatives to salt flakes. The meat will only take as much salt as it needs and any excess will fall off when it is flipped.

When it comes to seasoning before cooking, there are many schools of thought: some season the meat well in advance. It also depends on the cut of meat. Very generally, I like to season pork and chicken well in advance, by using either a wet or dry brine, but with bloodier meats such as beef steaks I tend not to season until at most an hour or so before cooking, as otherwise the salt can draw out too much blood.

PULLED PORK

brining : at least 12 hours, ideally overnight | *cooking : about 6 ½ hours*

for the pork:

1 whole pork shoulder butt

sugar, ¼ of the shoulder weight

salt, ¼ of the shoulder weight

3 tbsp brown sugar

for the jasmine rice:

4 cups rice, or ½ cup per serve

4 tsp jasmine tea leaves

8 cups water, or 1 cup per serve

2–3 cm / 1 in. knob of ginger

1 spring onion (scallion)

1 tbsp vegetable oil

1 tbsp chaoxing vinegar

salt or soy sauce, to season

to serve:

lettuce cups & kimchi

to make pork rinds

Trim skin of fat, cut into smallish pieces, then boil in salty water for 30 minutes. Drain, season, then refrigerate overnight. Shallow-fry for 2–3 minutes. Drain and season again, then serve.

facing page: *Pulled Pork*

IT'S HARD TO BEAT the combination of smooth, deeply-flavoured pork and crisp, fresh lettuce, held together in the hand and bitten into with a loud, satisfying crunch, followed by a mouthful of warm meat and the sweet notes of jasmine rice.

Pulled Pork is made from that part of the shoulder known as the 'butt'. A whole shoulder has two parts, the other being the 'picnic shoulder', but it is the marbled, meaty butt that is needed here. Bone-in is better, if available: when cooked, it has a deeper flavour than boned, and the juices used for basting will also be richer in flavour.

Pork shoulders can be purchased with the skin on or already removed, and it depends on how it is to be cooked. For Pulled Pork, the skin is not needed, so remove it if your butcher has not already done so. (You can use this to make pork rinds — see note at left.)

The pork also needs to be cured overnight, an essential step to ensure it will have the right texture: tender and melty, yet surprisingly intact. Pulled Pork should just hold together in delicious, moist shreds, then easily fall apart.

This recipe uses a dry brine, so a lot of sugar and salt (equal parts) is needed.

METHOD: First work out how much salt you need for the dry brine by simply weighing the shoulder butt and dividing by 4.

The combined weight of the sugar and salt should be half that of the shoulder.

Make sure the skin has been removed from the pork shoulder, and then rub the brine into the meat. Place in the fridge, uncovered, overnight, or for at least 12 hours. During that time, turn it once to ensure an even cure.

to bake the pork: Pre-heat the oven to 120°C / 250°F.

Meanwhile, take the pork shoulder from the fridge. Rinse off the salt and sugar, pat it dry, then place it on a rack inside a deep baking pan.

Allow it to cook very slowly for 6 hours, basting it every 30 minutes or so with its own juices.

At the 5½-hour mark, crank the oven up to 220°C / 425°F. Carefully take the pork out of the oven and massage in the brown sugar (as the pork will be hot, you may need to use heat-proof culinary gloves for this step).

Return the pork to the oven and allow it to bake further until the sugar has caramelized and it reaches an internal temperature of 95°C / 203°F. This should take 10–15 minutes or so.

Remove the pork from the oven once more and allow it to rest for 20 minutes before breaking the caramel crust and releasing the lovely aromas and the slow-cooked meat beneath.

Use two forks to gently pull at the pork in different directions to shred it.

to cook the rice: While the pork is resting, there's time to cook the rice.

First make the jasmine tea in the usual way: one teaspoon of leaves per serve and one for the pot, and then pour over the boiling water. Allow the tea to steep for 2–3 minutes.

Meanwhile, finely slice the spring onion (green and white parts), and grate the ginger.

Add to a pot with the vegetable oil, vinegar, and the rice, and then, using a strainer, pour over the jasmine tea. Place the pot over a medium–high heat and bring to a moderate simmer, but don't allow it to boil. Cook for a good 10 or 15 minutes, until all the liquid is absorbed, and add some extra water or tea if it looks like it might dry out.

Once cooked, remove it from the heat and allow it to rest for 5–10 minutes with the lid on. This will allow it to absorb any remaining moisture, to leave soft, fluffy rice.

Serve the warm Pulled Pork together with some jasmine rice and some kimchi (optional) inside the crispy lettuce cups.

Season with salt or a splash or soy sauce, if desired.

PORK *with* DUCK RILLETTES

preparation : *12 hours for brining* | cooking : *3½–4 hours*

for the brine:

brine solution (see note)

for the rillettes:

1 kg / 2 lb pork shoulder butt, boned

500 g / 1 lb duck fat

3 onions, peeled and sliced

2 heads garlic

1 tsp ground cardamom

3 cloves

2 whole duck legs

1 cup white wine

a few sprigs of thyme

1–2 bay leaves, fresh or dried

1 tbsp juniper berries

2 tsp black peppercorn

Brine

For this recipe, make a solution with lots of cups of water (enough to cover the pork) and 1.8% salt by weight. So, 1000 ml weighs 1000 g, so you would need 18 g of salt; 2 pints of water weighs 40 oz, so you'd need ¾ oz of salt.

RILLETTES IS DELICATELY shredded meat, such as duck or pork, that has been cooked slowly in its own fat until the fat and meat have melded together to become soft, rich, and spreadable. The word itself is derived from the Old French 'rille', meaning a slice of pork or poultry.

Unlike pâté, rillettes are not made from liver and nor are they a uniformly textured paste: the main similarity between the two is only that rillettes and pâté are both meat spreads. The melt-in-the-mouth texture of rillettes is a distinctive feature, as is its muted colours and wave-like peaks and troughs.

METHOD : At least 12 hours before your cook, prepare the brine by dissolving the salt in a large pot of boiling water. A full litre of brine (1000 ml or about 2 pints) should be enough, but it must fully cover the pork. If necessary, add some more water and salt to the correct proportions (1.8% salt to water, by weight, for this recipe).

Allow the brine to cool completely, and then add the pork. Cover and place in the fridge for up to 12 hours.

About 30 minutes before you are ready to make the rillettes, pre-heat your oven to 160°C / 320°F. While it is warming up, remove the pork from the brine, pat dry with paper towels (don't rinse it), and allow it about 30 minutes to come up to room temperature.

You should also have the duck legs ready to go. Keep back about 30 g / 1 oz of the duck fat, then place the rest in a baking pan and allow it to melt in the hot oven. Add the duck legs and the other ingredients including the pork, then bake very slowly for 3 hours, after which time the duck meat should be falling off the bone and all the meat very tender and floating in rich, brothy juices.

Remove from the oven and use a colander to drain off the liquid over another pot, to catch the juices and reserve them. Once that is done, gently tip the drained meat back into the baking tray and, using heat-proof culinary gloves, spread it out widely and loosely with your hands. Meticulously but quickly sift through it with your fingers to pick out any stems or twigs (from the herbs) and any berries (including peppercorns), cloves, bits of bone, and other matter except the meat. All that should remain is the soft, almost buttery, meat.

Season generously with salt and sherry vinegar. These flavours might seem quite strong at first but will mellow as the meat cools. Pour the reserved liquid through a fine sieve and then add 2–3 tablespoons to the meat: just enough liquid to coat all of the meat and then a little bit more, so that it is nicely moist and buttery.

Pack the rillettes tightly into sterilised jars, firmly pushing the mixture down and compressing to ensure there is no air. Very gently melt the remaining 30 g / 1 fl. oz of duck fat over a low heat, then pour over the top of the rillettes to form an air-tight seal. Allow to set in the refrigerator. Provided the rillettes was hot when poured into the jars (above 60°C / 140°F — use a thermometer to check) and properly sealed, it will keep for a month or two in the refrigerator, but once the fat seal is broken it should be eaten within 3 days. Don't be tempted to reheat the rillettes to bring the temperature back up again as it will alter the dish in various ways.

above: *restaurant work — picking through a large volume of rillettes*

above: *rillettes served with toasted baguette, grainy mustard, and watercress*

SMOKED PORK BELLY

curing: *24 hours* | preparation & cooking: *6–8 hours*

1 whole pork belly

2–3 tbsp olive oil

2–3 tbsp apple cider vinegar

for the dry brine:

100 g / 3 oz cooking salt

100 g / 3 oz raw sugar

1–2 tbsp juniper berries

1 tbsp black peppercorns

2–3 bay leaves

1 tbsp fennel seeds

1 tsp chilli seeds

for the rub

2 tbsp brown sugar

2 tbsp smoked paprika

1 tsp cinnamon

1 tsp garlic powder

1 tsp onion powder

1 tbsp freshly-ground peppercorns

1 tbsp salt

SMOKING MEAT AS WELL as vegetables and cheese is an intriguing and satisfying way to add flavour and preserve these foods. It takes time and observation, but that's where the fun lies. Plenty of people make a hobby of smoking foods in the same way that others make wine or preserves, experimenting with different flavourings in both the wood chips and the rubs they use, as well as the cuts of meat and so on. It works very well with fatty cuts, to give deeply flavoured, melt-in-the-mouth results, while leaner cuts will tend to dry out too much.

Smoked pork belly is a great choice because it is mainly the fat which takes on the smoky flavours, and it also stays beautifully moist. Curing the meat beforehand will help keep the moisture in and ensures it is seasoned thoroughly. This recipes makes use of both a wet brine and a dry brine, in the form of a rub (see notes on p. 129).

There are many different types of smokers available, from traditional ones that make use of charcoal and woodchips (my preference) to the at times more practical electric and gas alternatives. Some rules that apply to all are: use fire-proof gloves, cook outside in a safe place, allow plenty of time, and clean appropriately after use. Other than that, follow the instructions as provided by the manufacturer.

METHOD: Mix together the brine ingredients and spread that heavily over the entire pork belly. Next, place the pork in a tray and leave for 24 hours to cure in the fridge. Turn once or twice over this time, to help the curing process.

left: *pork belly with rub, ready for cooking*

The next day, first prepare your smoker. Depending on the type, this can take 25 minutes or up to an hour, but it needs to have a good coal base and be holding a temperature of 100–130°C / 210–265°F before cooking starts.

As it heats up, take the pork from the fridge and pat dry.

Mix together the rub ingredients and cover that evenly over the pork. Let the pork rest for about 30 minutes at room temperature.

Once the smoker is ready, you can place the pork inside, and then add a couple of soaked smoking blocks (which will slowly smoulder rather than burn) or smoking chips. Be sure there is a steady stream of clean smoke emitting from the smoker, and that the temperature remains steady for about 6–8 hours. As the pork crust begins to dry out, spray with slightly diluted apple cider vinegar every hour or so (2 parts vinegar to 1 part water works well) to keep the meat moist.

Continue to add smoking chips or blocks as needed over the first hour or so of the cook. The time will vary depending on size of the pork and heat of the smoker, but it is at this time the pork's internal temperature will rise from room temperature (20°C / 68°F approx.) to 50°C / 120°F approx. It's important to add the smoking chips at this early stage because it's when the meat and fat take on the smoky flavours. Once its internal temperature rises beyond a certain point, it stops taking on flavours.

Once the pork has reached around 70°C / 160°F (usually around the 3-hour mark, about two-thirds of the way through the cook) you will need to wrap it in butcher's paper or foil (see 'flatline' note), and then continue cooking for a few more hours until it reaches 95°C / 203°F. At this point, it should fall apart into rich, moist 'pulled pork'.

Dry brines and rubs

Both contain salt (usually: some rubs are salt-free), are made of dry ingredients, and are rubbed into various meats before cooking. Yet despite their similarities, their primary purposes are different. Brines season the meat throughout and are also for adding moisture. Rubs are used to add flavour to meat. If they also contain salt, however, that will assist in melting any fat in the meat as it cooks, to produce a juicier result. Additionally, if left on the meat for a few hours or more, a salty rub will begin to act in the same way as a dry brine, further contributing to a tender, succulent result.

The flatline

The 'flatline' of low temperature cooking is reached when evaporation of steam off the surface of the smoker cools down the meat, so it struggles to cook the meat further. For this reason, it is necessary at this point to wrap the meat to prevent cooling so it can continue to cook to the right temperature.

facing page: *Smoked Pork Belly*

PORK ROAST *with* CRISPY POTATOES, BALSAMIC RED ONION *and* CRACKLING

preparation: *12 hours if curing overnight, otherwise 3–4 hours* | *cooking: about 2 hours*

for the pork:

1 large rack of pork

1–2 tbsp olive oil, approx.

salt flakes, to season

for the dry brine

1 tbsp table salt, approx.

for the wet brine alternative

brine solution (see p. 123)

for the onions:

4–5 red onions, peeled

150 ml / 5 fl. oz balsamic vinegar

2 tbsp white sugar

2 tsp olive oil

for the potatoes:

60 g / 2 oz duck fat or 3 tbsp cooking oil

1 kg / 2 lb brushed all-purpose potatoes, peeled

1 head of garlic

4–5 sprigs of rosemary

salt flakes, to serve

FOR GREAT CRACKLING, the skin and fat must first be scored and the skin dried out in the fridge. 'Scoring' just means cutting through the skin and fat, but not all the way through to the meat below. These two steps are what make the crackling crisp up and separate into scrumptious — there is no other word – flaky, crumbly, lip-smacking bands across the crest of the meat. If you can get it, choose female pork because it has less of a smell than male and is also generally a better quality.

METHOD: To score the pork, use a small, sharp knife to cut the skin at 1 cm / ½ in. intervals across its width. The right depth will depend on the thickness of the skin and fat layers (usually around 1½ cm / ⅔ in.), and the scores should only cut about three quarters of the way through. I like to use a clean utility knife because the small blade helps control the depth of the scores.

overnight brining: You will get the best results if you marinate the pork overnight in a wet brine. It's not essential but can be what turns a good meal into a great one. So, after scoring the pork skin, make the brine as described on page 123. Once it has cooled completely place the pork in the brine, making sure it is fully submerged.

Cover and leave in the fridge overnight. The next morning, remove the pork from the brine, pat dry with a paper towel, and then leave it to dry, skin-side up and uncovered, in the fridge for a few more hours.

for a quicker preparation: If you are short of time, the pork will still benefit from a few hours' drying out. Just rub it all over with the table salt and place it in the fridge, skin-side up and uncovered, for as much time as you can before you start cooking.

to bake the pork and onions: Set your oven to a hot 250°C / 480°F. Take the pork from the fridge and rub it all over with olive oil, and then season generously with the salt flakes. Place it in a baking tray and allow 30 minutes or so for it to come up to room temperature.

Place in the oven and bake, while keeping an eye on the skin for crackling. In a very hot oven, this should start to develop at the 15–20 minute mark, and then continue to form over the next 20. If you think it needs some help, change over to a hot grill setting, to really focus heat onto the top layer of the meat. Watch that it doesn't burn.

Meanwhile, cut the onions into 1 cm / ½ in. slices. When you are happy with the crackling (it should look deliciously golden and bubbly) reduce the oven heat to 180°C /356°F. Toss the onions into the tray, alongside the pork, and allow everything to cook for another 40–50 minutes or so, until the internal temperature of the pork reaches 60°C /140°F and the onions are nicely softened. All up, it will take 1½–1¾ hours to cook the meal.

above: *the pork in the wet brine*

above: *Pork Roast, showing crackling but with the onions still to be cooked*

Take out the pork and place it on a carving board. Leave it, uncovered, in a warm spot for 10–15 minutes, to allow the crackling to 'vent' and crisp up a little more.

Separately, deglaze the onions with the balsamic vinegar and then add the sugar. Bake for a further 10–15 minutes, until the balsamic is sticky but still slightly runny and the onions are starting to caramelize.

to bake the potatoes: All-purpose potatoes (e.g., coliban, sebago, désirée) work best here because they will crisp up but stay fluffy inside. Allow about an hour — 10 minutes to par-boil, 45–50 minutes to cook — so make a start shortly after the onions go in the oven. This may be more than needed, but you can delay baking them if you over-did the par-boiling, or cover them in foil for a while to slow things down. It should work if you pop them in the oven about 15 minutes after the onions, but then keep an eye on them. They need to be ready at the same time as the meat (after it has rested).

First, cut them into roughly even-sized chunks: large ones into quarters, medium into thirds, and small into halves (leave the skin on if you like, although the potatoes might not crisp up as well). Place in a pot of cold, well-salted water, bring it to the boil, then reduce to a medium simmer to par-boil. They should just be starting to soften, so that you can insert a skewer, but there should still be some resistance. This should take 10 minutes or so.

Strain in a colander and return them to the pot. Give them a good shake to toss them around and fluff up the edges, to catch the fat and crisp up the outsides. If you've nailed the par-boil, the potatoes should fluff up evenly on the outside while remaining nicely intact. (If they don't, don't worry: smaller pieces will still be delicious). Spread the chunks out on a tray and allow them to steam up further as they cool down.

Meanwhile, as the potatoes are cooking, place the fat (or oil) in another baking tray and warm in the oven for at least 10 minutes. I use duck fat because it has a subtle yet rich flavour and produces crispy potatoes that are soft and fluffy inside. Vegetable oils with high smoke points also work well (grapeseed, canola, sunflower, etc.), and a dash of olive oil can be added to brighten the flavour. Some people roast potatoes in just olive oil, but they never seem to crunch up as much: not for me, anyway. Olive oil has a high smoke point, but it seems the potatoes soak it up too easily rather than allowing it to crisp up the edges.

Once the fat is hot, use a wide spoon to carefully slide the cool, drained potatoes into the fat and then gently toss them to coat. Check on them every 15 minutes or so, tossing them again each time, until they are beginning to turn a golden brown but have not yet crisped up. This will take at least 30 minutes, maybe a little longer.

Smash the garlic head into cloves, and, leaving them unpeeled, crush with the back of a knife. Toss in with the potatoes, together with the rosemary and roast for a further 20 minutes, or until the potatoes are crunchy. Season with salt flakes then serve.

above: *roast potato with rosemary*

above: *potatoes in duck fat, with herbs*

LAMB LOIN *with* SALSA VERDE *and* POTATOES

brining : *2–24 hours* | cooking : *about 2 hours*

for the lamb:

1 boneless lamb loin

1 garlic clove, peeled, optional

2–3 tbsp rub

for the salsa verde:

1 bunch each continental parsley, coriander (cilantro) & dill

1 green chilli

2 tbsp capers, rinsed

anchovies, finely sliced, to taste, optional

1 tbsp olive oil, approx.

zest and juice of 1 lemon

2–3 tsp sherry vinegar, to taste

salt, to season

for the potatoes:

200 g / 7 oz all-purpose potatoes

1 tsp bicarbonate of soda

3 tbsp cooking salt

100 g / 3 oz duck fat

4–5 rosemary sprigs or finely-sliced chives

6–8 unpeeled garlic cloves

FOR ME, ROASTED OR GRILLED LAMB has always been a staple and favourite meal. When I was growing up, my mother would serve a beautifully roasted leg of lamb with baked vegetables every Monday evening. It was always superbly cooked, caramelized on the outside and delicately pink within, and perfectly complemented by a slightly sweet, slightly acidic, refreshing mint sauce (which she usually made, fresh, rather than using a bottled variety). Sometimes there would be gravy, too.

When my family moved to the Middle East for my father's work, I discovered lamb cuisine that was simultaneously rustic, sophisticated and delicious. Lamb was used in sweetly-spiced tagines that were baked for many hours in lidded, earthenware pots (the 'tagines'), until melt-in-the-mouth tender and piping hot; whole lambs were cooked over flaming spits, to then be finely carved and served with any number of spiced and usually garlicky accompaniments; and sambouseks, small triangles of filo pastry filled with spiced minced lamb, were a favourite street food but also served at restaurants.

It was in South America that I found how irresistible hot roasted lamb could be when served with cool salsa verde, or with chimmichurri (p. 178). There's something about the slightly earthy flavours of the lamb that's enhanced by those of the fresh but earthy salsa verde or, by contrast, complemented by the singing notes of a zinging chimmichurri. This recipe uses salsa verde, but chimmichurri can be substituted for an equally rewarding result (but I would serve that with a salad, not potatoes).

To make the rub

Mix together a couple of teaspoons each of suitable dried herbs (such as rosemary, thyme, and oregano), a heaped teaspoon of salt, and a good grinding of pepper. Be generous with the salt as it also helps the rub to act as a kind of brine.

Timing is important. You need to massage the rub into the lamb first, and then allow at least 2 and up to 24 hours for brining: longer is better. The potatoes will take 1–2 hours to cook. Use your judgement here, but it is worth allowing more time than expected: potatoes will cope with a bit of over-cooking, and if you are worried they are cooking too quickly you can drop the heat back and cover them with foil to slow the process down, and then crank up the heat again later (see Method for more details).

METHOD: This recipe uses a dry brine, or 'rub', to prepare the lamb before cooking. It is a good idea to mix your own, so you can control the flavours, but if pressed for time pre-made ones also work quite well: just be careful their flavours will work with the dish, not against it.

to prepare the lamb: Trim off any excess fat and rub all over with the garlic clove (if using), then thoroughly massage in the dry brine. Place it in the fridge uncovered, and leave for at least 2 hours and up to 24, and then remove from the fridge about 30 minutes before you begin cooking it.

to bake the potatoes: Pre-heat the oven to 200°C / 392°F. Place the duck fat in a deep baking tray and put it in the oven to warm up as you prepare the potatoes. This should be done about 2 hours before you are ready to serve, to allow plenty of time for the potatoes to cook.

Peel the potatoes and cut them into roughly even-sized pieces: large ones into quarters, medium into thirds, and small into halves. If you have lots of small, even-sized potatoes, you can leave them whole.

Place them in a pot and cover with cold water then add the salt and bicarbonate of soda and bring to the boil, then reduce the heat and simmer for about 3 minutes. Drain and pat dry with paper towels.

Once the duck fat is hot, take the pan from the oven and carefully spread the potatoes through the fat. Gently shake the pan a little, to toss the potatoes through the fat, and then return the potatoes to the hot oven. Turn the potatoes every 20–30 minutes or so throughout the cook until they are crispy, and add the rosemary and garlic 20 minutes before you're ready to serve.

to roast the lamb: Meanwhile, take the lamb from the fridge and bring it to room temperature (about 30 minutes). After the potatoes have been in the oven for an hour, pop in the lamb. Bake it on a rack in the oven alongside the potatoes until it reaches an internal temperature of 55°C / 131°F. Then remove it from the oven and allow it to rest for 5–10 minutes in a warm place. The temperature will climb higher.

to make the salsa verde: De-seed the chilli and remove the larger stems from the herbs. Using a sharp knife, slice the chilli and herbs to a fine texture (rather than using a blender as you don't want to bruise them), then place in a large bowl. Season to taste, then add the capers and a pinch of the anchovy (if using). You can also try adding more anchovy or a touch of soy sauce instead of salt to add layers of flavour. The salsa should be slightly acidic, which will cut through the lamb fat. Cover with olive oil and vinegar: the usual ratio is 1 part vinegar to 2 parts oil, but it depends on personal taste.

to bring it together: Carve the lamb into thin slices, drizzle with the salsa verde, and serve alongside the crispy potatoes, topped with salt flakes.

above: *salsa verde*

above: *slicing the lamb loin*

above: *serving lamb*

RACK *of* LAMB *with* HONEY GLAZE, DUTCH CARROTS *and* BEETROOT PURÉE

preparation : *about 30 minutes* | cooking : *about 30 minutes*

1 rack of lamb

for the marinade:

handful of fresh coriander (cilantro)

2 garlic cloves, peeled

50 g / 1¾ oz clear honey

25 ml / 1 fl.oz lemon juice

50 ml / 2 fl.oz soy sauce

for the beetroots & carrots:

3–4 large beetroots

2 tbsp butter

50 ml / 2 fl.oz cream

1 bunch dutch carrots

1–2 tbsp olive oil

2 tsp caraway seeds

salt, for cooking and seasoning

pepper, to season

I HAVE SERVED THIS DISH, many times, and people always bring their plates back for more. It can be made at any time of the year, but spring is best because that is when the lamb is young and tender and the flavour at its most delicate. It is beautifully marinated in a spiced mixture sweetened with honey, and served with dutch carrots, with an earthy beetroot purée to finish.

METHOD: Trim any excess fat off the lamb and set the oven to high (220°C / 430°F) so it will have time to heat up.

to put together the marinade: After first removing the larger stems from the coriander (cilantro), roughly chop the leaves and also crush the garlic cloves. Mix these in with the remaining marinade ingredients and then massage the marinade into the lamb.

Allow the meat to sit at room temperature for 10–15 minutes so the marinade can work its magic.

to make the beetroot purée: Give the beetroots a quick rinse and then place them, unpeeled, in a pot and cover with cold, salted water. Bring to the boil and then reduce to a gentle simmer.

Cook until the beets are soft but not mushy (about 20 minutes, depending on size — sometimes they take a lot longer). Once cooked, drain the beetroots and allow them to cool enough so you can use your fingers to rub off the skin. You can use a knife or peeler if you prefer, or to remove any stubborn bits, but that can take too much off as the beetroots will be quite soft.

Once that is done, place them in a food processor or blender together with the butter and cream and blend until smooth. Season with the salt and pepper to taste and, if you are seeking an elegant, smooth purée, pass it through a fine sieve. It comes down to personal preference and even the time and place (sometimes a slightly chunkier, rustic version will work better).

Place it in the fridge until you are ready to serve.

to prepare the carrots: Trim the tops off the carrots and discard. Toss the carrots, washed but unpeeled, in the olive oil together with the caraway seeds and a pinch of salt, so they are ready to pop in the oven later.

to bring it all together: Now place the marinated lamb in a baking tray and roast it in the pre-heated oven. Add the carrots at the same time, in the same pan. If they are very small, you might need to cover them with foil so they don't burn, and just remove the foil a couple of minutes before you are ready to take the lamb out of the oven.

Baste the lamb every 5 minutes or so as it will only take 15–20 minutes to cook. To check, insert a meat thermometer into the thickest part of the lamb. It can be taken out of the oven when the internal temperature reaches 62°C / 143°F. Allow it to rest, covered in a clean tea towel, for at least 5 and ideally 10 minutes. Leave the carrots in the oven so they stay warm, but drop the oven back to about 160°C / 320°F so they don't over-cook.

Carve the lamb and serve together with the carrots and puréed beets and pan juices.

above: *fresh beetroots from the vegetable garden*

above: *rack of lamb roasting in the oven*
following page: *Carlotta Arch mountainside of Jenolan Cave, Blue Mountains, New South Wales*

Pasta | Pizza | Polenta

PIZZA DOUGH

preparation: *1-3 days*

for the starter:

10g / ⅓ oz fresh yeast

100ml / 3½ fl. oz water, at room temperature

100g / 3½ oz strong flour

for the dough:

700ml / 2½ fl. oz cold water

1 kg / 2 lb high-protein flour

20 g / ⅔ oz salt

1 tbsp honey

20 ml / ⅔ fl. oz olive oil

semolina flour, for dusting

THERE ARE LOTS OF WAYS to make pizza dough, and people often develop their own recipes over time.

When it comes to cooking, the pizza bases can be baked in a very hot conventional oven or pizza-maker, but for me I like to cook them outside in my home-built pizza oven, using a dough made from a fresh yeast starter. This gives the simple rustic flavours that I like so much, as well as the right crispiness to the pizza base that forms on the hot oven floor. This dough also rolls out nice and thinly, while staying strong enough to support the toppings.

It takes a bit more time to make than simpler recipes that use instant or dry yeast, but it's worth it. The preparation is part of the whole experience.

The science behind bread-making, including pizza dough, is quite involved, but there are three key details behind it all. First, when flour is moistened and then kneaded, gluten is formed. This is what gives dough its elastic, or stretchy, qualities. Gluten also hardens on cooking and so provides bread and other cooked doughs with the structure to hold their shape. Second, yeast is a living organism that produces gases (carbon dioxide) as it consumes the sugars (broken-down carbohydrate) in the dough. This gas expands in pockets between the strands of gluten, to make the dough rise, and also make it fluffy when cooked. Third, fermentation and dough-making processes produce certain bacteria that add flavour, texture, aromas and also nutritional benefits.

facing page: *pizza dough and assorted toppings*

METHOD: At least a day ahead of baking, make your starter by mixing the fresh yeast with the water until it dissolves. Stir through the flour all at once, and then leave the mix for 5 minutes before stirring once again. Cover and refrigerate overnight.

The next day, start by sanitizing a big tub with boiling water. This will be your 'fermentation vessel' and it needs to be clean.

Measure out the cold water and pour it into the tub, and then add the starter. It should have risen overnight while in the fridge, and a good sign that it is ready to use is that it will float when dropped in the water. This is known as the 'float test'.

Add the high-protein flour and give everything an initial mix using very clean hands. Once it is just mixed, add the salt and then work the dough until it fully comes together. This will take a few minutes and a bit of elbow grease.

There are two similar but separate steps that follow: bulk fermentation and proofing, both which entail leaving the dough to sit as it rises. For the first step, shape the dough into a ball and cover the outside with about half of the olive oil. Rub it around the dough as this will prevent the outside from drying out, and then return it to the tub. Wet and squeeze out a clean tea-towel and place it over the top.

Every 30 minutes, take out the dough and stretch it out (to about twice its width) then fold it back over onto itself, and then return it to the tub and cover with the tea-towel again. Do this for the next 2 hours or so, until it becomes very smooth and shows signs of rising. At this point, you can choose to let the dough fully rise if you want to use it soon. Or, you can put it back in the fridge for up to 48 hours, which is about the ideal time for pizza dough to ferment. Refrigeration slow downs the fermentation process by slowing the activity of the yeast, allowing more time for the bacteria to develop. It is that which produces a more flavoursome dough.

When you are almost ready to use the dough, divide it into roughly six 280 g / 10 oz portions. Shape each into a smooth ball and dust lightly with semolina flour then spread them out on a semolina-dusted tray so they have room to prove (rise) once, slightly. I like to use semolina flour for dusting because it is coarse and doesn't change the hydration or form sticky clumps in the way that other flours do – but if you don't have any to hand, plain flour will do. The dough balls should increase by about a quarter or so in size. They are then ready to be stretched out into pizza bases and baked, or they can be stored in the fridge, covered in clingwrap for 2–3 days. After that, the gluten will be 'exhausted' and the dough more likely to break. See the instructions for baking the pizza bases on page 154, along with suggested toppings.

left: *the finished outdoor oven, at Taralga, in New South Wales*

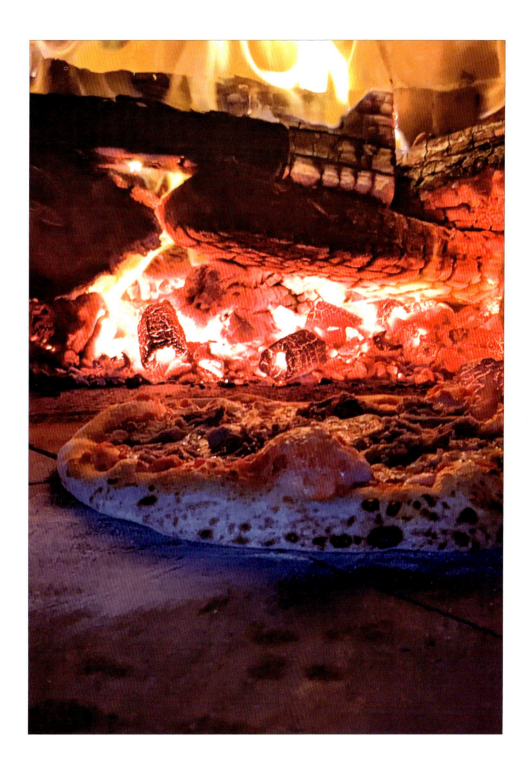

facing page: *the building stages of the oven*
above: *firing pizza in the oven*

PIZZAS!

heating: *30 minutes–3 hours* | **preparation & cooking:** *15–30 minutes, excluding dough-making*

Suggested toppings:

Margherita
cook: San Marzano Sauce,
mozzarella
top with: garlic oil,* dried
oregano, & salt

Neapolitana
cook: San Marzano Sauce,
mozzarella
top with: bocconcini, torn basil
leaves, garlic oil, salt & pepper

Capricciosa
cook: San Marzano Sauce,
mozzarella shaved ham,
portobello mushrooms,
artichokes, olives
top with: dried oregano, pepper,
salt, & fresh rocket

* Garlic oil
Lovely drizzled over hot pizza —
add 2–4 crushed garlic cloves to a
½ cup of olive oil. Warm gently for
a few minutes, until the garlic is
soft and slightly coloured. Strain
and refrigerate, and then use
within 3–4 days.

FOR ME, BAKING PIZZAS in an outdoor wood-fired oven is the best way to capture wonderful rustic flavours. Biting into them in the brisk outdoors — straight from the oven, crispy-based, and steaming hot — is part of the whole joyous experience, as is staying warm close to the cosy oven as they bake. So, pizza-baking works best in the winter and autumn (fall) months, and it is also a wonderful family or social activity — but they can be enjoyed at any time of year.

using a conventional oven: If you don't have an outdoor pizza oven, the next best option is to bake your pizza on a pizza stone on the highest setting your oven can manage — 230°C / 450°F gives the best results. Give the stone a good half hour to heat up in the oven before baking. A wood-fired oven will take much longer — at least 3 hours.

Of course, before heating your oven you will need to have already prepared your pizza dough, at least a day ahead (see p. 149). While the oven heats up, about 30 minutes ahead of baking time, you can start preparing the tomato base, if using (see San Manzano Sauce, p. 181). You can also cut up and otherwise prepare your toppings. It is nice to have them chopped roughly into bite-sized chunks, then placed in bowls so you can easily grab small handfuls and sprinkle them over the bases when needed.

using an outdoor wood-fired oven: If you are baking in one of these, you will need to allow at least 3 hours for the heat to fully soak into the bricks. The first step is always safety: have a large bucket of water or fire extinguisher on hand to douse the fire if it starts to get out of hand (this is unlikely, but where fire is concerned it is necessary to be prepared, just in case). Also use fire-proof gloves to protect your hands. Use proper fire-proof utensils to add wood and to stoke the fire, and for dropping the pizzas into the oven when you are ready to bake.

If your oven does not have a temperature gauge, it is important to invest in a laser thermometer: it is a safe way to check oven temperatures from a distance.

To heat the oven, consult the manufacturer's manual for specific instruction regarding your model. That said, the general principles are:

First, open the oven door and the smoke vent. Scrunch up some newspaper (or other suitable wastepaper), place it in the middle of the oven floor, and build a tepee of kindling (usually 5–6 thin, dry pieces of wood and maybe some twigs and fire cones) over the top. You can also add a firelighter or two, but use natural, chemical-free ones to avoid unpleasant flavours and odours.

Light the fire and allow the kindling to catch. Once it is properly alight, gradually add more wood to build up the fire over the entire oven floor. This will take some time, but it is quite a meditative and enjoyable experience. Start by adding more kindling and smaller logs then slowly increase them in size.

Keep going until the oven temperature has climbed to around 350–400°C / 650–750°F. The oven is now ready for baking the pizzas and should stay hot for at least 2 hours or more, depending on the oven's thermal capacity.

The next step is to allow the fire to die down a little so that you can safely, using proper equipment, move it to the back of the oven and clear a space on which to cook the pizzas. Make sure smoke doesn't build up inside as the fire settles down, and leave the oven door open at all times (the presence of flames should limit the amount of

Pepperoni
cook: San Marzano Sauce, mozzarella, pepperoni, garlic oil
top with: pepper

Supreme
cook: San Marzano Sauce, mozzarella, red onion, capsicum, salami, mushroom, olives
top with: dried oregano, fresh rocket, garlic oil, salt & pepper

Pulled pork, Apple & Honey
cook: San Marzano Sauce, mozzarella, pulled pork
top with: freshly sliced apple, chilli honey,* fresh rocket, & salt

Roast Capsicum, Squash & Goats Cheese
cook: San Marzano Sauce, mozzarella, parmesan, mandolined squash, roast capsicum
top with: fresh goats cheese, salt & pepper

*Chilli honey
An tantalising condiment: just simmer a ½ cup of honey, a teaspoon of chilli flakes, and some salt and pepper for 1 minute. Take off the heat and add a tablespoon of apple cider vinegar. Cool before transferring to sterilised jars. It should keep for a few months

smoke). The pizzas need a raging fire to cook properly, however (so don't let the fire die down too much because you will then need to build it up again before you start cooking).

The trick to this is to place a smallish log on the hot bricks in the cleared area a minute or so before you want to start cooking the pizza, so it heat ups but does not catch alight. Just before you place the pizzas in the oven, very carefully shift the log onto the fire at the back of the oven so it ignites immediately and cranks up the fire.

making the pizzas: Dust down a work bench with a generous dusting of flour (semolina flour works best as it won't become sticky). Roll out the balls of pizza dough until they are each about 3 mm / ⅛ in. thick.

I usually split the toppings into two: those that are to be cooked in the oven (generally, the sauces, cheeses, meats, and vegetables) and toppings that are added later, just before serving (herbs, seasonings, condiments, etc.). It can vary though with, for example, some cheeses such as bocconcini and goats cheese being added after cooking rather than before. Suggested toppings are given on the previous pages, but always play around with your own preferred ingredients and see what works best for you. Whatever combinations you use, avoid making the toppings too thick or using too much cheese: neither are necessary and they take away from the delicious balance between the flavour and textures of both the dough base and the toppings.

Once the pizzas are assembled, one at a time slide a pizza peel (or paddle) underneath and then drop the pizza onto the cleared space on the oven floor. Depending on the size of the oven and pizzas, you may be able to cook 2–3 at a time, but don't crowd them. Keep a good space between them, not least so you can manouvre the pizza peel and take them out easily once they are cooked.

Provided your oven is properly heated and is at prime temperature, the pizzas should only take 90 seconds or so to cook. Keep an eye on them: they should have a firm but crispy base that will support the other ingredients (check this by sliding a pizza peel underneath and having a quick look). It is also a good idea to rotate them — carefully — in the oven so they cook evenly. The rest of the dough should be slightly puffy, golden, and even slightly charred in places, cheeses nicely melted and sauces gently bubbling. If they are not quite ready, give them another 30–60 seconds or so. Baking might take a little longer if you are using a conventional oven, depending on how hot that can get.

Once ready, use the pizza peel to slide each pizza out of the oven, place onto a chopping board, sprinkle with the remaining toppings, and then cut into slices and serve.

facing page: *freshly-baked pizza ready to serve*

left to right: *stretching the dough, getting ready to place pizza in the oven; firing the pizza; ready to serve*

FOCACCIA

poolish: *1–24 hours* | mixing and baking: *1½–2 hours*

for the poolish:

400 g / 14 oz strong bakers flour

400 ml / 14 fl. oz cold water

8 g / ⅓ oz fresh yeast, or 1⅓ tsp dry yeast

for the dough:

1 kg / 2 lb strong bakers flour

760 ml / 1⅓ pints tepid water, about 25°C / 77°F

1 tbsp salt, approx.

2–2½ tbsp olive oil, approx.

salt flakes, to serve

Some suggested toppings:

thinly sliced onion, whole pitted olives, & rosemary sprigs

confit garlic, with or without some grated parmesan

whole cherry tomatoes & torn fresh basil leaves

mandolined potatoes, crushed garlic, & rosemary sprigs.

caramelized onion

grated parmesan & rosemary sprigs

FOCACCIA CAN BE TOPPED with various flavourings of your choosing: experiment, and see what works. Personally, I like to use some thinly sliced red onion, whole pitted olives and rosemary. Cherry tomatoes also work well, as do combinations of garlic and herbs. Many people also add cheese, but I avoid adding too much as it can dominate the subtle flavours and textures of the baked dough and turn it into a sort of airy pizza — which isn't really the point here. Traditionally, focaccia can have cheese in the topping or not, but if so generally only a thin layer.

Sometimes, toppings such as pitted olives or small lardons of bacon and other suitable ingredients are studded into the top of the focaccia before baking.

The dough itself is quite easy to make, starting with the 'poolish'. This is a starter dough or 'pre-fermenter' that includes yeast and which is added to the main dough later. This gives the dough its flavour characteristics — quite earthy and wholesome but less sour than sourdough — as well as its enticing aromas. It also helps the fermentation process, which in turn forms lots of bubbles that results in an airy texture when the dough is baked.

The poolish method originated in Poland in the mid 1800s but then became popular in Austria, France, and further afield (the name 'poolish' is derived from 'polonais', the French word for 'Polish'). A similar but drier and more solid starter dough known as 'biga' was developed in Italy at roughly the same time (in the 1800s) and used to make pizzas and focaccias. Of course, those baked goods date back centuries but were, in earlier times, flatbreads. Biga

facing page: *putting together potato and rosemary pizza*

above: *focaccia dough, brushed with oil (top) and topped with rosemary, cherry tomatoes, and onion (above)*

is still used today, but poolish can be used instead and has the advantage of needing less time to ferment. It will also produce a crispier crust and smaller air bubbles. By contrast, biga is an essential ingredient in ciabatta, the Italian bread with large holes and an almost waxy texture. This would not be achievable if poolish were used instead.

METHOD: There are five key steps spread over time: making the poolish, making the dough, fermenting the dough, proving it, and then finally baking.

to make the poolish: Using a wooden spoon, mix together the poolish ingredients in a tub or large bowl. Cover and leave at room temperature for about 10 minutes.

Mix again, and then cover and leave at room temperature until it has doubled in size. This will usually take an hour or so at room temperature. A lower temperature will cause it to rise more slowly, but that will also impart more flavour into the final product. How long to leave dough to rise is really a matter of watching it rather than timing it, because there are so many variables at play (how strong the poolish was, the quality of the ingredients, the ambient temperature, and so on).

Once it is ready, you can begin making the dough immediately, or put the poolish in the fridge overnight if you are wanting to bake the following day: longer is better, if you have the time.

to make the dough: Place a large bowl on kitchen scales and begin by adding your water. Next add in the risen poolish. To test that the poolish is ready, drop some into the water; it should easily float.

If not, the pre-fermentation process is not complete and you will need to put the poolish in a warmer environment and allow it more time.

Once the poolish has been added to the water, add the flour all at once and give the dough a quick stir. Just as it begins to combine, add the salt and oil. Now ditch the wooden mixing spoon, wash your hands, and get in there and knead the dough until it comes together. At this point it doesn't need to be completely smooth.

Once the dough is brought together, cover with a wrung-out wet tea towel and leave on the bench at room temperature for half an hour or so.

Then, starting at one edge of the dough, pull it upwards as far as it will go without breaking and then fold it over itself. Now rotate the dough, and pick up the next edge and repeat this step. Repeat the process until you have gone around the edges of the dough two or three times, by which time it should be smooth, then place the dough back on the bench and cover the surface with some more olive oil so that it doesn't develop a skin

Leave the dough to 'bulk ferment' — this refers to the first time the dough rises and it is a critical step in the process. It should at least double in size, and again this will take an hour or so (see notes on previous page). Once there, oil up a deep baking tray and transfer the dough across. Then use your fingers to press the classic focaccia dimples into the dough.

Cover again with a moist tea towel and set your oven on high (250°C / 480°F).

Meanwhile, allow the dough to 'prove', which is the second time it is left to ferment and increase in size. You should see some significant growth in the dough by this point and, once it looks bubbly and risen you can then dimple the dough again and add your preferred toppings (see list of suggestions).

baking the focaccia: Now pop the dough in the oven. To make it rise further, place a small baking tray with a thin layer of water on a lower oven rack, to encourage steam. Bake it for about 15-20 minutes until golden brown.

Allow it to cool slightly before slicing and serving with a good sprinkling of salt flakes.

above: *focaccia dough with olives and rosemary, ready for baking*
facing page: *baked tomato, onion, and rosemary focaccia*

CARBONARA MAFALDINE

preparation & cooking : *about 30 minutes*

200 g / 7 oz guanciale

1 brown onion, peeled

3–4 garlic cloves, peeled

salt & pepper, to season

150 ml / 5 fl. oz white wine

200 g / 7 oz mafaldine pasta

1 whole egg

4 additional yolks

150 g / 5 oz grated parmesan

2 tsp freshly ground black pepper, or to taste

handful of fresh parsley

extra parmesan, to serve, optional

1–2 tbsp olive oil, optional

additional salt flakes & pepper, to season

SOME SAY the term 'Carbonara' comes from 'carbonaro', the Italian word for 'coal burner', and that it may have developed as a meal made quickly and easily from readily available ingredients by the 'carbonari', or Italian coal burners, in times past. True to this history, it is a simple, humble dish, pulled together from ingredients close at hand. It gains much of its flavour from gianciale, a rich, melt-in-the-mouth cured meat from Central Italy, made from the cheek of a pig.

Traditionally, guanciale is not smoky in flavour (as the name of the recipe might misleadingly suggest) but rather is rich, salty (less so than pancetta), and even slightly sweet.

Mafaldine pasta originates from the south of Italy, in and around Naples. It is ribbon-shaped, with curled edges to catch the creamy sauces and which also give an attractive presentation. Made from durum wheat and water, it is typical of the pastas from southern Italy, while those of the north will usually include egg. It is said to have been named in honour of Princess Mafalda of Savoy (1902–44), the second daughter of King Victor Emmanuel III of Italy, although it is also said it was popular well before her birth but was known by a different name.

In the south of Italy, seafood is a staple, more so than in the northern regions where beef, pork, game and other meats are more common. Hence variations of this recipe that substitute seafood for the guanciale, often known as Carbonara di Mare, are commonplace. The addition of cheese would be far less likely as, generally speaking,

facing page: *serving the Carbonara Mafaldine*

above: frying the guanciale, boiling the pasta, with the parmesan and egg ready to go

cheese and seafood are not mixed in Italian cuisine. Mafaldine pasta itself, though, is often served with seafood dishes. Guanciale can be hard to source, in which case pancetta or even bacon can be substituted. This dish also needs a generous amount of parmesan.

METHOD: Dice the guanciale into 1 cm / ½ in. lardons and then fry them in a large, dry pan over a medium-high heat, until the fat begins to soften and becomes more translucent around the edges.

Finely dice the onion and add it to the pan. Continue to cook, stirring occasionally, for about 5 minutes, until the onion has softened and has begun to take on a gentle colour.

Crush the garlic and add it to the mix. Cook for a few moments until just aromatic, then season with the salt and freshly ground pepper.

De-glaze with the wine and allow a few moments for the sharp scent of alcohol to cook off, and then reduce the heat to medium. Simmer until the sauce has reduced to about half its original volume. This will take 3–5 minutes.

Meanwhile, bring a large pot of well-salted water to the boil. It should almost taste like the ocean, quite salty. Add the pasta and cook accordingly (about 1–2 minutes for fresh pasta, and about 9 minutes for dry). When cooked, it should have a gentle bite, but there should be no white left in the centre. Don't start cooking the pasta before your sauce has properly reduced, as both need to stay hot for the next step.

As the pasta cooks, mix the eggs, parmesan, and black pepper together in a large bowl. Separately, trim the stems off the parsley then finely slice the leaves.

Drain the cooked pasta and toss it heavily through the egg and cheese mixture to form and emulsify the sauce.

It is important to work quickly so the hot pasta gently cooks the egg without scrambling it. Allowing the heat of the pasta to cook the egg (rather than the heat of stove) is an essential step, as is the special way in which the starch from the pasta and the egg emulsify to create the distinctive sauce. It is also why carbonara dishes are so beautifully creamy: less pasta plus sauce; more pasta and sauce as one.

To finish, toss through the parsley then serve with a fresh grating of parmesan and a generous glug of extra virgin olive oil, if desired. Season to taste with more freshly ground pepper and salt flakes.

POLENTA

preparation & first cook: *1–24 hours, depending on cooling time* preparation : *10 minutes*

1½ litres / 3 pints chicken or vegetable stock

1 litre / 2 pints milk

500 g / 1 lb polenta

2 cloves garlic, peeled

1 cob of raw corn, grated

120 g / 4 oz shaved parmesan

salt & white pepper, to season

olive oil & butter as needed, for frying

herbed yoghurt or aioli, to serve, optional

DECADES AFTER my great-grandfather Nello died, he was remembered with a deep fondness and respect by the older Italian chefs, restaurateurs, and waiters around Melbourne. Apparently, this made it much easier for his many descendants to secure a table at popular Italian restaurants on short notice. It still does, on occasion.

One simple dish he made was polenta: hot and fluffy on the inside and crispy on the outside. Later, my grandfather Bart would hanker for it, but he could not find a suitable recipe. He conducted many experiments, with the first attempts resulting in a puddly mush before he invested in a miniature grill to toast the polenta into shape — but he was always disappointed with the results. Most likely, he didn't allow the cooked polenta time to cool down and firm up enough before frying: impatient by nature, he probably couldn't be bothered with that step and didn't want to wait.

I also add some grated, raw corn to the mixture, which provides extra texture and some sweetness. This might be the influence of my time living in Texas and South America, where corn is a staple, sneaking into the recipe.

METHOD: In a large pot, bring the stock and milk to a gentle boil. Add the polenta and use a whisk to stir it through the liquid. Whisk thoroughly so the polenta hydrates evenly.

Continue cooking out the polenta, whisking constantly for about 15 minutes until it thickens. Turn the heat down if it is boiling too heavily, as otherwise it will start to spit. Once it is thick crush the garlic and add it to the mix, followed by the grated corn and parmesan. Season to taste. It will have formed a gruel and can be enjoyed, served hot and 'as is', or portioned and stored for later use.

to portion the polenta: Line a large tray with baking paper. Pour in the polenta and spread evenly. Alternatively, pour the polenta into lighty-greased ramekins. Cool in the fridge for at the very least half an hour (3 hours is better) and preferably overnight.

to fry the polenta: Once cold, flip the polenta out onto a chopping board. Remove the paper and cut the polenta into batons, or whatever shape that you like.

If pan-frying, heat some olive oil and butter in the pan. Once sizzling, drop in the batons, a few at a time. Fry until crisp and golden, turning as needed. Alternatively, they can be deep-fried. Once crisp and golden, drain onto paper towels. Season and serve hot with herbed yoghurt, aioli, or any other compatible accompaniment of your choice.

to bake the polenta: If baking batons, place them in a single layer on a lined baking tray. Brush the tops lightly with olive oil then place in a 200°C / 390°F oven. Bake for about 10 minutes then turn them over. Brush the tops with olive oil and cook for another 10–15 minutes until crisp and golden. Drain on paper towels, season, and serve hot.

to bake polenta in moulds: Place in a 180°C / 350°F oven for a good 20 minutes so that the polenta warms through and becomes drier as it bakes. Insert a skewer to check, as you would with a cake: it should come out clean, ideally with a little puff of steam. Brush the tops with olive oil, then crank up the oven or put the ramekins under the grill for a few minutes, just long enough to crisp up the tops, then serve. One restaurant I know of on the Mornington Peninsula tips the baked polenta from the mould into a bowl, then pours a hot Napoletana sauce around the sides, like a hot, red moat.

above: *polenta chips*
following pages: *winter near Laggan, New South Wales*

Condiments | Sauces | Something Sweet

ONION JAM

cooking : *about 1 hour or a little longer*

8 brown onions, peeled

1 tbsp olive oil

2 tsp brown sugar

2 in. knob of ginger, grated

½ tsp turmeric

2 cups port

25 ml / 1 fl. oz red wine vinegar

1–2 tsp additional butter

THIS SAVOURY, SWEET, and sticky jam is mouth-wateringly delicious served with warm grilled meats and also with cheese and chacuterie.

I use brown onions because they caramelize well and have an earthier flavour. White onions can also be used, but the flavour will be sweeter, and red onions are often less successful.

Whichever you use, slice them finely but not too finely or they will burn or become mushy. They must be cooked very slowly to achieve a rich caramelization.

Make sure that you use a heavy-based large pot, so the onions are not piled too deep and can cook down evenly.

METHOD : First slice the onions into 3 mm / ⅛ in. rounds.

Next, melt the butter over a very low heat. It shouldn't sizzle or foam.

Some people add olive oil as well, to stop the butter burning, but it shouldn't be necessary if the cooking temperature is sufficiently low.

Add the sliced onions to the pot and leave them to caramelize slowly (very, very slowly, more than you would expect) over 45 minutes, or maybe an hour or more. They won't need much attention, but check them every 15 minutes or so and give them a little stir if needed.

You can cover them with a lid in the early stages as this will help to prevent them from sticking.

Once they have reached a nice golden colour, add the brown sugar, ginger and turmeric and continue cooking over a low heat for a further 20 minutes or so.

Add a third of the port to the pot and stir it through the onions.

Increase the heat to medium-high and allow the jam to reduce back to the original volume (before the port was added). Then repeat this step twice, so that all the port is used.

Add a small knob of butter and stir through the vinegar together with a pinch of salt. Once it has been fully incorporated, remove the jam from the heat.

It can then be transferred while still hot to a sterilized preserving jar, taking care not to shock the glass (see note at right). The jam will keep in the refrigerator for up to 3 months, noting that the sugar and vinegar will help to preserve it.

Avoid shocking the glass

There is some risk of 'shocking' glass jars, causing them to shatter. This happens when there is too sudden a change of temperature, such as when hot liquids are poured into cold jars. To avoid this, warm the outside of the jars under running hot water for a few moments (being careful not to touch the sterilized interior), before pouring in the hot liquid.

above: *Onion Jam*

BRONWYN'S PESTO

preparation: *about 10 minutes*

2 cups fresh sweet basil leaves

¼ cup pine nuts

¼ cup olive oil

2 tsp lemon juice

2 cloves garlic, peeled

1 tsp salt

¼ cup parmesan, grated

2 tbsp romano cheese, grated

PESTO IS A CONDIMENT that originates from Italy, most particularly the Liguria region (of which Genoa is the capital) where it is often thickened with goats cheese to make a thick, heavy sauce that is served with gnocchi and green beans. Less creamier versions, where the main ingredients are basil leaves and olive oil, are found all over Italy and bear many similarities to the French condiment of similar name, pistou.

This is my mother's recipe for pesto. It was a staple condiment used in many a family meal and even as a simple spread as my two brothers and I grew up in various parts of the world. My father's work meant we relocated to different countries many times, but pesto was a reassuring constant, always available, and always delicious.

My father remembers his own father Bart setting out on a search for fresh basil in the suburbs of Melbourne in the early 1970s, so that he could replicate the pesto made by, in turn, his own father, Nello, many years earlier. Without the availability of online searches at that time, Bart's search proved fruitless, so he instead eventually managed to order, by mail, seeds from which to grow his own. Growing basil then became a hobby for Bart, and he would patiently wait for the soft, young leaves to appear before rinsing and drying them and making his own pesto.

He would then finely chop the leaves, using what he called a 'lunetta' or small moon, the double-handled moon-shaped knife more commonly known as a 'mezzaluna', or half-moon. It is a widely-used utensil today but he probably located it, after some searching, in one of the many small shops run by Italian immigrants in Melbourne's inner north in the 1960s and '70s. Once the pesto was made, it would be stored in the fridge in glass jars, always covered with a film of olive oil, where it would keep for many weeks.

Bart was particular about the need to scrape down the sides of the glass jars above the level of the pesto and to ensure the pesto was fully covered by oil, so it would not spoil. He was also extremely particular about the basil to be used: it had to be young, so the leaves soft and the flavour delicate. And it had to be 'sweet basil', not one of the hotter or more peppery varieties. As soon as the basil had 'gone to seed', he declared it unusable as the flavour would be bitter, and then expelled it from his garden.

These days, given the ready availability of basil leaves, it is probably best to make pesto and use it as needed. This means there is no risk of it spoiling, which can sometimes happen with foods that include pine nuts, cheese, garlic, and similar ingredients.

METHOD : Place all the ingredients except the lemon juice together in a food processor (a powerful jug blender will also work) and blend on high speed to the desired consistency. Transfer the pesto to a bowl and stir through the lemon juice just before serving (this will preserve its bright green colour).

above: *Bronwyn's Pesto, freshly-made*

CHIMMICHURRI

preparation: *about 10 minutes*

1 bunch continental parsley

2 red chillies

3–5 garlic cloves or to taste, peeled

⅓ cup olive oil, or to taste

2 tbsp sherry vinegar, or to taste

salt & pepper, to season

1 tsp honey

1 tsp soy sauce

CHIMMICHURRI IS A SPIRITED, SPICY SAUCE, or salsa, from Argentina. I was introduced to it when growing up in Texas but I later learnt to perfect it, under the instruction of the Argentinian chef Francis Mallmann. The addition of honey and soy is untraditional: just a fun 'bump' created while I was playing around with a fellow chef when in Chile (we called that version 'Bobbychurri').

Chimmichurri's greatness lies in its simplicity; without interference, it allows the contrasting flavours and textures of fresh ingredients to blend in the mouth. It is as if the sauce itself is alive: simultaneously refreshing and hot; sweet yet sour; textured but smooth. A dash of chilli is all that's needed to provide the kick to this culinary dance.

When served with grilled (or barbecued) meats, its tangy juices swirl in with those smokier ones from the meat, to create a mouth-watering and tantalising combination.

The parsley and chilli must be sliced very finely and cleanly, not chopped or puréed. The slices don't have to be a uniform size, either; it's good to include some larger pieces that end up being cut by the teeth upon eating, to release an incomparable burst of flavour. Sometimes a food processor or blender is used, but it doesn't work as well because they bruise and crush the parsley and chillies too much, causing them to lose their vibrant character, in terms of colour, texture, and taste.

It has some similarities to salsa verde but excludes the earthier, brinier flavours of anchovies and capers. It is traditionally served over barbecued, grilled or roasted meats such as beef, chicken, lamb and fish (less so pork), but it can also be used as a marinade prior to grilling, as a spread or dip, and even mixed through pasta, in a similar manner to pesto. It is at its best eaten within a few hours of making, to allow just enough time for the flavours to meld while still retaining a fresh brightness to its colour and flavour. Use sparingly: a small amount goes a very long way.

METHOD: Remove the larger stems from the parsley and, using a sharp knife, chop it finely by hand. Slice rather than crush, so it stays green, and then place it in a large bowl

De-seed and finely slice the chilli, then grate the garlic over the top. Roughly mix the garlic and chilli together, and, using your hands, mix that lightly through the parsley. Be sure to combine the garlic and chilli first, rather than adding them directly to the parsley, because that will allow the distinctive garlic-chilli flavour to properly develop.

Now mix together the oil and vinegar, making sure you have enough to fully cover the parsley. A quarter cup of oil and 2 tablespoons of vinegar is a good start, then adjust as needed. Use a ratio of 2 parts oil to 1 part vinegar, and then tweak according to taste.

Next cover the parsley with the oil and vinegar then season with salt and pepper. Taste again, and add a little more vinegar if you want a sharper flavour, which works very well with fattier cuts of meat. As a very subtle flavour enhancer, mix the honey and soy in a small bowl until the honey has dissolved and stir through just before serving.

above: *Chimmichurri*

above: *San Marzano sauce in the making*

SAN MARZANO SAUCE

preparation: *5–10 minutes*

2.2 kg / 5 lb tinned San Marzarno tomatoes, or thereabouts

3–4 tbsp olive oil

40 g / 1¼ oz garlic, peeled – about 8–10 cloves

2 tsp black pepper

3½ tsp salt

small bunch of fresh basil leaves

SAN MARZANO TOMATOES are a plum-shaped variety. They are longer and narrower with a pointier tip than others of this type. They also have a superior flavour that balances intense umami notes against their sweeter ones, and they are often recommended for canning or bottling. They come from the Campania region in southern Italy, a 'Protected Designation of Origin' based on the volcanic soils in which they are grown. Hence, the chances of finding authentic, fresh San Marzano tomatoes outside of Italy are slim, although 'descendants' are grown from seeds in other locations. Canned ones are available through various commercial brands.

I love to use this sauce as the tomato base in my pizzas, leaving it uncooked to give it brighter, fresher flavour. It then receives all the gentle cooking it needs once placed in the hot oven. It should be made just ahead of using, so that the flavours stay fresh, but otherwise will keep for a day or two in the fridge or can be frozen for later use.

METHOD: Crush the garlic and then mix all the ingredients together in a large container. The traditional way is to use your hands to squish the tomatoes through your fingers, leaving chunkier pieces in the mix so you get that burst of fresh tomato flavour. Otherwise, you can use a stick blender on its lowest speed to gently blend the ingredients. The aim is not to have a fully emulsified and homogeneous sauce, but rather one where the tomatoes are broken up enough just to make it spreadable.

AIOLI

preparation : *10 minutes*

4 cloves garlic, peeled, or 1 tbsp garlic confit (see p. 38)

2 eggs yolks

1 tsp dijon mustard

1 tbsp apple cider vinegar

300 ml / 10½ fl. oz vegetable oil

salt flakes, to season

Mayonnaise

To make, just omit the garlic in this recipe. Because there are no lumps of garlic to be pulverized, it can be made quickly with a hand or electric mixer, and there's no need to sieve it. Herbs such as finely sliced dill, chives, and parsley are often added after blending, and lemon can be used instead of or as well as vinegar.

THIS IS A LOVELY, RICH accompaniment to various salads as well as hot and chilled dishes. It is basically a mayonnaise with garlic added to the ingredients.

METHOD : Roughly chop the garlic, and then place all ingredients except the oil and the salt into a jug blender or food processor.

Blend on a medium–high speed as you very slowly begin to drizzle in the oil through the hole in the lid. As the mixture begins to thicken, drizzle in the remaining oil until the mixture reaches a thick, creamy consistency.

For a luxurious finish, pass the mixture through a fine sieve then season generously with salt. Use a teaspoon or so – more than seems necessary, but it will be worth it.

Allow the mixture to stand for about 10 minutes before serving.

It will also keep in a covered container or jar in the fridge for about 3 days, after which any left-overs should be discarded. It is not suitable for freezing.

HARISSA

preparation & cooking : *about 30 minutes*

2 red capsicums

10 red chillies

1 tsp cumin seeds

3 cloves garlic, peeled

1 tsp smoked paprika

2 tbsp lemon juice

2 tsp red wine vinegar

3 tbsp olive oil

salt flakes, to season

I WAS FIRST INTRODUCED to this hot, flavoursome paste at the street stalls and markets of Qatar, where I lived with my family from the age of 9 until 14. It is a traditional condiment that originates from Northwest Africa and the Middle East (the 'Maghreb').

The best and most authentic versions are made by charring the skin of the chillies and capsicum over an open flame. Ideally, freshly toasted cumin seeds should also be used, rather than a pre-ground cumin powder which, although technically the same ingredient, will have a less intense flavour.

METHOD: To char the capsicum, keep them whole and spear them with a barbecue or roasting fork. Place them over a low, open flame, about 2–3 cm away, so they are not in direct contact (or place them on a hotplate over the flame) and carefully rotate them until they are nicely blistered and charred all over.

Be careful not to over-do it, or they will burst, burn, or overcook. The flesh inside should be soft and plump, not burnt or dehydrated. Charring should take about 5–10 minutes, depending on size of the ingredients, and can be done outdoors over a campfire or barbecue flame, but also indoors over a gas hotplate.

Once charred, place the capsicum in a bowl and cover tightly with cling film so they sweat. Allow at least 10 minutes: this will deepen the flavours and also make them easier to peel later.

facing page: *charring chillies on a barbecue hotplate*

The chillies can be charred in a similar way, but much more quickly (about 1–2 minutes). Use a skewer or smaller fork to hold them over the flame and watch them carefully. When they are ready, add them to the bowl with the capsicum and cover again with the film. Leave for a minute or two to sweat and until cool enough to handle.

Meanwhile, toss the cumin seeds into a hot, dry pan over medium-high heat and toast for just 10–15 seconds, constantly swirling the pan or stirring the seeds so they don't burn (which they can do, very easily and very quickly: watch them the whole time). Once the aromas are prevalent, (which is when their aromatic oils are released), tip them out onto a sheet of baking or parchment paper. Allow them to cool.

Add the toasted cumin seeds and the remaining ingredients except the peppers and chillies to a blender. Blend on a high speed to form a smooth paste. If you have an older or less powerful blender, it may help to grind the seeds in a spice grinder or crush them lightly with a mortar-and-pestle first, and to roughly chop the garlic.

Separately, de-seed the peppers and chillies and use your fingers to rub off the blistered skin. Use a small, sharp knife or a vegetable peeler to remove any remaining bits. Next add the flesh to the blender. Blend well with the other ingredients, and then adjust the seasoning as needed. A little more vinegar can also be added at this point, according to taste.

From here, the harissa can be taken in many directions. It is a great accompaniment to grilled seafood, chicken and beef, and for charred vegetables and other nibbles off a barbecue. It can also be mixed with mayonnaise (see p. 183). to make a delicious dressing for salads and sandwiches (mix about 2 parts mayonnaise to 1 part harissa), and even added to baked dishes such as tagines or served alongside grilled prawns.

above: *Harissa*

ROMESCO SAUCE

preparation: *about 15 minutes*

4 red capsicums

2 tomatoes

1 red chilli

100 g / 3 oz toasted almonds

2 cloves of garlic

25 ml / 1 fl. oz red wine vinegar

50 ml / 1¾ fl. oz olive oil

1 tsp paprika

salt, to season

THIS SMOKY CONDIMENT from Spain is used as a sauce for grills, as a spread or a dip, and even as a spoonful of extra flavour to serve with soups and various other dishes. Its smokiness is integral to its flavour, so it works best when cooked over the open flame of a wood fire.

METHOD: First prepare your firepit, barbecue, or wood-fired oven. Then, in the early stages when the flames are roaring, take the time to (very carefully) char the skins of the capsicum, chilli and tomatoes, until they are blistered and burnt. It's easiest to do one or two at a time, using tongs to hold them over the flame, and turning as needed. As each one is done, put it in a bowl and cover with cling wrap, and then allow it to steam up as you cook the rest.

When the last is done, put that in the bowl with the others, cover again with the clingwrap, and wait until they have all cooled. You can then peel off the skins and remove the seeds. It's often easier to use your hands to peel and rub of the skins while pushing the seeds away and using your fingers as a sort-of sieve to catch the flesh — but do this over the bowl as it will be messy, transferring the flesh to a blender or food-processor as you go. Otherwise, use a small knife to peel the skins and scrape away the seeds, but that is usually slower — and not as much fun.

Add the remaining ingredients to the vegetable flesh and blitz well to the desired consistency. If you want a chunkier sauce, put the peeled and de-seeded flesh in a bowl and roughly purée with a stick blender, or even mash with a fork or potato masher for a rustic finish.

BASQUE CHEESECAKE

preparation & cooking : *45-50 minutes*

7 medium eggs

1 kg / 2 pounds cream cheese

400 g sugar / 13 ⅓ oz sugar

2 cups cream

1 tbsp almond flour

I LEARNT how to make this wonderful, burnt-topped cheesecake while attending a cooking course in San Sebastian, Spain, around the time of my 23rd birthday. Over the years I've strived to perfect it and to highlight the contrasts between the sweet, rich (very rich) creamy interior and the slightly bitter, burnt crust.

I use almond flour so that it is gluten-free, but you can substitute plain flour if you prefer. It is a favourite of mine and a real crowd-pleaser.

METHOD: Pre-heat your oven to 230°C / 446°F, ensuring both top and bottom heating elements are turned on.

Break the eggs into a large bowl and beat well.

Using a stick blender, mix the cream cheese in with the eggs, until well combined.

Fold through the remaining ingredients, one at a time, with a wooden spoon, beginning with the sugar, followed by the cream, and lastly, the flour. Ensure each ingredient is mixed in well before adding the next.

Finish by blending for a further 30 seconds or so, to create a very smooth consistency.

Line a springform pan with baking paper so that the paper peeks over by at least 5 cm (a couple inches) above the rim of the pan because the cake will rise.

Pour the mix into the pan and bake in the oven for approximately 30-40 minutes.

facing page: *Basque Cheesecake in the baking pan*

The cake is ready when it has risen, is well burnt on top, and is still quite wobbly within the pan, but not jiggly.

To test this, while the cake is still in the oven give the pan a gentle rap. The cake should wobble slightly and then stabilise. If it jiggles, it needs to be cooked for longer Another way is to use a thermometer to check the internal temperature; the cake will be ready when it reaches 66°C / 150°F — but that's not as much fun as watching the wobble.

above: *Basque Cheesecake, ready to serve*

CHOCOLATE MOUSSE

making & setting time: *2 ½ hours*

10 eggs, separated

100 g / 3½ oz caster sugar

300 g / 10½ oz dark chocolate (76%)

1 tsp butter, approx.

1 tbsp vanilla essence

Bain maries & double boilers

A bain marie is a water bath generally used to melt foods that might otherwise burn or spit if the heat is too intense. Double-boilers can also be used for this purpose. They comprise two parts: a lower pot and then a suitably-sized heat-proof bowl (large enough so it can sit on top but not fall in). To make a double-boiler, place not more than 5 cm / 2 in. of water in the base of a pot and bring it to a low boil. Sit the other bowl with the ingredients on top. Always ensure there is at least 10 cm / 4 in. of clear space between the water level and the base of the bowl above it, to avoid risk of shattering.

A FOOL-PROOF RECIPE for this always-popular dessert.

METHOD: Whisk the yolks heavily with the sugar until pale Gently melt the chocolate in a bain marie.

Once melted, fold the chocolate into the egg mix along with the vanilla and a soft but not melted knob of butter. Mix together thoroughly but gently.

Separately, whisk the egg whites to a firm peak. Next, gently fold them, one third at a time, into the chocolate-and-yolk mixture. Be careful to retain as much air in the whites as possible and do not over-mix at this point.

Pour into moulds and allow to set in the fridge for at least 2 hours before serving. This recipe does not require gelatine.

above: *Chocolate Mousse in the making*

ACKNOWLEDGEMENTS

The authors express their thanks to Brolly Publishing for their support and commitment to this project, and also to the many people who have contributed in various ways. First, to Sophie Purser and the local Central Tablelands community for all the fresh produce they have provided for Simon's cooking. Sophie's contribution to the photography and her work in styling is also gratefully acknowledged, as is the support of Simon's colleagues who have shown a keen interest throughout this book's development. Thanks is also due to Bridgette Adam for her editorial and proofreading support. There are so many others, including family members, friends, and associates, who have provided input and helped in the shaping of this book, to which deep thanks are also extended.

ABOUT THE AUTHORS

Simon Borghesi is a highly qualified and experienced chef who has travelled the globe honing his skills since childhood. Recognised for his passion, talent, and skill, he has trained under some of the world's great chefs while building his repertoire and developing his own style. He is currently Head Chef at Matt Moran's The Rockley Pub.

Luisa Adam is a writer and publisher with over 30 years' experience in trade, academic, and government publishing. She holds a Masters in Editing and Publishing and a second in Design and has also written several books. In the early 2000s, she founded her own publishing company which is now run as a family concern.